CROSSROADS

OTHER BOOKS OF INTEREST

From DEMERS BOOKS (www.demersbooks.com)

John Fenton Wheeler, *Last Man Out: Memoirs of the Last U.S. Reporter Castro Kicked Out of Cuba During the Cold War* (October 2008).
ISBN: 978-0-9816002-0-8 (paper)

Charles Merrill, *Colom: Solving the Enigma of Columbus' Origins* (October 2008).
ISBN: 978-0-9816002-2-2 (paper)

From MARQUETTE BOOKS (www.marquettebooks.com)

John W. Cones, *Dictionary of Film Finance and Distribution: A Guide for Independent Filmmakers* (2008). ISBN 978-0-922993-93-2 (cloth);
978-0-922993-94-9 (paper)

Hazel Dicken-Garcia and Giovanna Dell'Orto, *Hated Ideas and the American Civil War Press* (2008). ISBN: 978-0-922993-89-5 (cloth); 978-0-922993-88-8 (paper)

Eric G. Stephan and R. Wayne Pace, *The 7 Secrets of Successful, Happy People* (2008). ISBN: 978-0-922993-75-8 (paper)

R. Thomas Berner, *Fundamentals of Journalism: Reporting, Writing and Editing* (2007). ISBN 978-0-922993-76-5 (paper)

Tomasz Pludowski (ed.), *How the World's News Media Reacted to 9/11: Essays from Around the Globe* (2007). ISBN: 978-0-922993-66-6 (paper);
978-0-922993-73-4 (cloth)

Stephen D. Cooper, *Watching the Watchdog: Bloggers as the Fifth Estate* (2006).
ISBN: 0-922993-46-7 (cloth); 0-922993-47-5 (paper)

Ralph D. Berenger (ed.), *Cybermedia Go to War: Role of Convergent Media Before and During the 2003 Iraq War* (2006). ISBN: 0-922993-48-1 (cloth);
0-922993-49-1 (paper)

Jami Fullerton and Alice Kendrick, *Advertising's War on Terrorism: The Story of the Shared Values Initiative* (2006). ISBN: 0-922993-43-2 (cloth);
0-922993-44-0 (paper)

Mitchell Land and Bill W. Hornaday, *Contemporary Media Ethics: A Practical Guide for Students, Scholars and Professionals* (2006).
ISBN: 0-922993-41-6 (cloth); 0-922993-42-4 (paper)

CROSSROADS

THE LIFE AND AFTERLIFE OF BLUES LEGEND

ROBERT JOHNSON

TOM GRAVES

FOREWORD BY STEVE LAVERE

DEMERS BOOKS LLC
SPOKANE, WASHINGTON

PRINTED IN THE UNITED STATES OF AMERICA

Except where noted, all photographs and illustrations in this book
are in the public domain and were obtained from the
digital collections housed online at the Library of Congress.

CATALOGING-IN-PUBLICATION DATA

Graves, Tom, 1954-
  Crossroads : the life and afterlife of blues legend Robert Johnson / Tom
  Graves ; foreword by Steve LaVere.
    p. cm.
  Includes bibliographical references (p.) and index.
  ISBN 978-0-9816002-1-5 (pbk. : alk. paper) --
  1. Johnson, Robert, d. 1938. 2. Blues musicians--Mississippi--Biography.
  I. Title.

                                                          2008925674

Edited by Darcy K. Creviston

DEMERS BOOKS LLC

5915 S. Regal St., Suite 118B
Spokane, Washington 99223
509-443-7057 (voice) / 509-448-2191 (fax)
books@demersbooks.com / www.DemersBooks.com

For Allison, Bintou and Mom

CONTENTS

STRAIGHT TALK

By Steve LaVere

Tom Graves' *Crossroads* is perhaps the most accurate recital of facts concerning Robert Johnson's life and death that you're likely to come across for many years to come. A large portion of this volume also deals very clearly and objectively with Johnson's phenomenal afterlife, in which his place in the pantheon of major artists of the 20th century has grown from being acknowledged initially as "The King of the Delta Blues Singers" (itself a remarkable attribution for one whose initial output was a mere dozen 78 rpm recordings) to being one of a few watershed artists in the entire history of music. Mr. Graves covers it all, from Johnson's initial appearance on long play records — a time when very little was known about him — through his life, including the discovery of the few photographs of him, the resurgence of interest in him after those discoveries, and the search for the rightful heir to the small fortune that had amassed from the royalties collected from the use of Johnson's songs.

Graves' book contains less hyperbole and more factual information about Johnson than any other book on the market. Nearly every major article or book previously published about Johnson contains major flaws — either the research was faulty and unsubstantiated or it was rife with false ideas, romantic exaggeration or myths that were treated as fact. Graves' book carefully separates fact from fiction, dealing with the romanticism, exaggeration and myth without disguise. In addition, he presents, for the first time, the truth concerning Johnson's poisoning, his death-bed conversion, the cause of his death and the location of his burial. There's also a decisive exploration of the snippet of silent motion picture footage that was initially touted as being Johnson but was subsequently proved not to be him.

However, this book does not so much destroy the myths about Johnson as it removes the myths from the realm of possibility, then deals with them for what they are. Despite some peoples' lamentations that myths give people hope and make life more interesting, Johnson's music itself is enough to create its own world of hope, one where all of us — especially blues fans — can appreciate musicians who make us think of the world and other people in a whole new way. In addition, one could point out, as Graves does, that even the destruction of myth doesn't signal the destruction of culture or an appreciation of the people who actively create culture.

There is, indeed, a great deal of interesting reading here. But it wasn't always that way. By the time Frank Driggs' intriguing liner notes to the first reissue album of Robert Johnson's classic blues recordings, *King of the Delta Blues Singers*, eventually fired my imagination and motivated me to look into what real information there might be extant about the album's subject, I had already gleaned what little there was from the unsubstantiated accounts in inaccurate books by would-be researchers and short bits and articles in specialty magazines by well-intentioned fans.

The liner notes, however, provided some good clues, so I began my search for Johnson where Johnson himself began, in Robinsonville, Miss. I got lucky and within a few weeks I was learning about the entire life and death of Robert Johnson from one of the best sources of a man's history: his sister, Carrie Thompson, who was closest to him throughout his early life. She took me into her confidence and disclosed a great deal of information not only about her precious "Little Robert" but every other member of her large, extended family as well. I wrote down everything she told me and later verified and documented everything I could from various census and civic records. I then re-foliated Robert Johnson's family tree back to the early 19th century. The exercise not only fleshed out Johnson as a man, including his background and life and death, it also brought into sharp focus my own concern for facts — a concern that is also shared by Tom Graves.

FACT, MYTH
AND THE MUSICIAN

Fifty years ago fewer than 100 people in the world knew anything of substance about the life of bluesman Robert Johnson. He died penniless and virtually unknown outside the Mississippi Delta. On the strength of twelve 78 rpm records he cut for American Record Corporation in 1936 and for Vocalion record label in 1936 and 1937, a legend began to percolate among an elite group of music folklorists and scholars who had begun to take "race" music — the music of African-Americans — seriously.

Robert Johnson's music first reached a wider audience in 1938, when legendary record producer John H. Hammond held a historic concert at Carnegie Hall in New York. The concert was called "From Spirituals to Swing," and introduced to the *haut monde* of New York the best and most varied of African-American musicians, composers and singers. Robert Johnson was listed on the concert bill, but he had died in August. On stage that night, John Hammond inaccurately told his audience, "Johnson died last week at the precise moment ... he was booked to appear at Carnegie Hall on December 23." He then played two of Robert Johnson's songs on a phonograph that was miked through the public address system.

Even after this landmark introduction to a world audience, almost no one knew anything of the life of the man himself. In later years, as Johnson's popularity grew, an army of blues researchers combed the Mississippi Delta for clues that would shed light on the real man. Most found the search maddening, because so little information could be found. Johnson remains one of the most elusive and mysterious figures ever accorded the status of a biography. Separating fact from fiction, legend from truth, accuracy from exaggeration is a Sisyphean task. Just when one fact seems verified, it is contradicted by other facts, other research.

Three biographical works on Robert Johnson, each with a unique and valuable perspective, were the cornerstones of wisdom and information for this book and were consulted frequently. They were *Searching for Robert Johnson* by Peter Guralnick, *Robert Johnson: Lost and Found,* by Barry Lee Pearson and Bill McCullough, and *Escaping the Delta,* by Elijah Wald. Also indispensable were the liner notes to the CD box set *Robert Johnson: The Complete Recordings,* written by Steve LaVere, who also wrote the foreword to this book. Robert Gordon's article, "The Plundering of Robert Johnson," was a valuable resource for the chapter on the discovery of Robert Johnson photographs. Anyone interested in delving deeper into the world of Robert Johnson should seek these texts. In addition, many other sources, including three documentary films, were used as references in the preparation of this book. They are listed in the bibliography.

This book, unlike most of the other materials produced about Johnson, was not written for scholars, ethnomusicologists or blues purists. It was written for people who simply love and appreciate music, especially the blues. My goal was to write a book that anyone could appreciate, so that is why I have taken the liberty to give the reader some basic background on what "blues" is and was (see Introduction). That isn't to say I don't welcome readers with extensive blues collections that include all 42 of Johnson's recordings. My hope is that after reading *Crossroads* novices will be able to connect the dots between blues, jazz, rock and roll, country and western, and even hip-hop.

If this book makes readers want to turn back the hands of time and listen to some of the classic recordings of Johnson, then I have done my job. If they figure out the pathways and connections — the continuum — from the music of *then* to the music of *now*, then I have done my job well.

ACKNOWLEDGMENTS

The body of research on Robert Johnson is much smaller than most people realize. Although there is a glut of minor, often conflicting, details, there are dismayingly few confirmed hard facts. Many writers have been guilty of embellishment and mythologizing. Many bluesmen who knew Johnson also have pandered to journalists and historians, giving false or misleading anecdotes because they didn't want their visitors to leave empty-handed.

That is why researcher Steve LaVere must be singled out for special thanks here, because, as I see it, he has applied the most stringent standards to the facts and history of Robert Johnson and has done the most to separate the truth from the hyperbole. The initial research he did in the 1970s for the aborted Robert Johnson box set laid the groundwork (whether he got credit for it or not) and allowed the rest of us to build on a very solid foundation.

I did not come into personal contact with LaVere until my book was completed, and I sought permission from him on my publisher's behalf for the rights to use one of the two surviving photographs of Robert Johnson for the cover of this book. LaVere was cordial and willing to help. I also found him to be reasonable, receptive, and wholly professional when it came to the business side of things. He carefully sifted through the pages of this book and made a great number of insightful suggestions.

Full disclosure compels me to alert readers to two areas regarding Robert Johnson where LaVere and I philosophically differ. As a result of his own research, LaVere concludes that Robert Johnson did in fact drink whiskey poisoned with strychnine yet did not die directly from it. He believes that Johnson, in his weakened condition, contracted a fatal case of pneumonia, for which there was no cure in the 1930s. Secondly, LaVere argues that the crossroads legend regarding Tommy Johnson did not jump from one bluesman to the other, but that Robert Johnson's crossroads allusions derived from his own life. As evidence, LaVere cites an interview with Willie Coffee and Johnson's mentor Ike Zinermon, who said he (Zinermon) learned to play guitar while sitting on tombstones at midnight in graveyards.

Peter Guralnick's book *Searching for Robert Johnson* also set a standard for the rest of us to follow, both in its scholarship and elegance of writing. I thank him for permission to use a quote or two from his book and for his thoughtful correspondence.

I also want to confer my deepest appreciation to my early readers, who always encouraged me yet didn't hesitate to let me know when I erred: my old, dear friend Jim Newcomb (the world's greatest line editor), Tom Carlson, Margaret Skinner and John Wilkinson. I also want to thank Robert Gordon for his help and attention, and biographers/researchers Elijah Wald, Gayle Dean Wardlow, Barry Lee Pearson and Bill McCullough.

Others who helped beyond the call of duty were Dr. David Evans, recording engineer Steven Lasker, my brother Norris Graves, my brother-in-law Moustapha Ndiaye, photo archivists Greg Johnson and Shugana Campbell at the University of Mississippi, Leo "Tater Red" Allred, guitarist Buddy Merrill, Phil Jones, Steve Nichols at the Shelby County Medical Examiner's Office in Memphis, Hawaiian guitar expert Lorene Ruymar, Howard Speir, Faye Speir Watkins, John Sale at *The* (Memphis) *Commercial Appeal*, Lauren Sposato with the United States Postal Service, photographer Bill Steber, photographer and musician St. Louis Frank, guitarist Calvin Newborn, Fred Jasper with Vanguard Records/Welk Music Group, Inc., filmmaker Robert Mugge and writer/critic Ed Ward.

Tom Graves
Memphis, Tennessee
January 2008

THE LOWLAND MISSISSIPPI DELTA PLANTATION BLUES

Summertime could be hell on the sprawling, low-lying cotton plantations in the flat bottomlands of the Mississippi Delta during the 1920s and 1930s. The sun could boil the sweat right out of a black man plowing behind the backside of a long-eared mule. Too much rain and the thick mud made plowing near impossible and brought out swarms of mosquitoes carrying misery and fevers. Too much sun and the crop would burn up, and the biting flies and gnats would take up where the mosquitoes left off.

If you were a bit lazy on the job, the boss man would be on your back and the landowner might dock your already subsistence wages. Strong arms and strong backs were a dime a dozen in the Mississippi Delta, and few of the workers, almost all of whom were descended from West African slaves who had worked those same fields, didn't dream of something better. Times were tough, especially during the Great Depression, and jobs were scarce, even for the educated whites who lived in the bigger cities. Soup kitchens and bread lines fed thousands of Americans, black and white and brown and yellow, who might otherwise have starved. For black farm laborers in Mississippi, there seemed little hope beyond ten thousand rows of white cotton.

Ten thousand rows of white hell is what life was like for field hands in the Delta cotton fields during the Great Depression of the 1930s. It was a life Robert Johnson wanted no part of.

But music provided some respite from the harsh reality. Sunday was a time of praise, joy and celebration for those who had found religion. Singing was one way they communicated worldly pain and evil to a God who understood their suffering. But for those who preferred the wilder side of life, Saturday nights offered pleasures and trouble, often in equal measure.

A black man working the fields of Mississippi all week long could find a good time at any number of shotgun shack clubs — "juke joints" — that were overflowing with music, dancing, gambling and alcohol. If he was a decent-looking man and carried a roll of cash in his pocket, he might even have his pick of women. Monday mornings the farmhands would be back in the fields, looking at a mule's hindquarters, but those Saturday nights took them into another world — a world where the rules for African-Americans were completely rewritten.

Those good times, however, often came at a high price. Streetwise cardsharps could easily cheat a naïve country boy out of

Gambling was a popular, and occasionally dangerous, activity in the 1930s at juke joints, such as the one pictured here in Clarksdale, Miss.

his wages at the gambling table. Getting "liquored up" spurred jealousies, brawls, knife fights, gunplay and on occasion cold-blooded murder. Parchman Farm, the notorious state penitentiary in Parchman, Miss., housed a fair number of black prisoners who had stepped over the line of common sense one time too many at a juke joint. Lots of songs were written about Parchman Farm by those who spent hard years there. The music that was most popular with African-Americans during this period defies easy classification. But blues was near or at the top of the list for most.[1]

---

[1] *The Oxford Companion to Music* defines blues as "typically a three-line stanza, the first line ... is ... repeated while the singer extemporizes the third, rhyming, line, and this is supported by a conventional 12-bar harmonic scheme: four bars on the tonic (two accompanying the first line), often with a flattened 7th in the 4th bar; two on the subdominant (accompanying the 2nd line); two more on the tonic; two on the dominant 7th (accompanying the rhyming line); and a final two on the tonic."

A Saturday night at a Clarksdale, Miss., juke joint in 1939.

Many historians argue that the term *blues* was first popularized around 1914 by the African-American composer and bandleader W. C. Handy, who published and performed "St. Louis Blues." However, many fans today would find his style closer to the sound of military marching bands than Delta blues. Handy led a full, uniformed band, and his instrument was the cornet, which is virtually unheard of in today's blues music. In his autobiography, *Father of the Blues*, Handy confessed that the original inspiration for his blues came after he heard a rural Southern black man playing a guitar at a train station. He described the scene this way:

> A lean, loose-jointed Negro had commenced plunking a guitar beside me while I slept. His clothes were rags; his feet peeped out of his shoes. His face had on it some of the sadness of the ages. As he played, he pressed a knife on the strings of the guitar in a manner popularized by Hawaiian guitarists who used steel bars. The effect was unforgettable. His song, too, struck me instantly.
> "Goin' where the Southern cross the Dog ..."

The singer repeated the line three times, accompanying himself on the guitar with the weirdest music I had ever heard. The tune stayed in my mind.

The tune stayed in his mind long enough for Handy to put down on paper a song called "Yellow Dog Blues" based in part on what he had heard at that train station. "Yellow Dog Blues" became another of Handy's great successes. To the buying public of the Roaring Twenties, a decade after Handy

W.C. Handy, standing in the middle of his large brass band, is considered by many to be the father of the blues.

published and popularized his first songs, blues had evolved and very probably conjured an image of a sassy song sung by a big-voiced belter such as Bessie Smith, who wowed audiences with songs like "Down Hearted Blues." Her style of blues, similar in some respects to New Orleans jazz, sounds little like the deep Delta music modern audiences now associate with pre-War blues.

Smith and blues queen Ethel Waters often sang songs containing double-entendre adult humor as a sort of naughty wink to their sophisticated, hip audiences, and then they could turn around and sing a popular Tin Pan Alley show tune favored by whites. Even in the most remote juke joints in Mississippi, where, as the cliche has it, they had to ship the sunshine in, jukeboxes carried a surprising cross section of music, from jazz and blues numbers to show tunes to white country hoedowns like those heard every week on the Grand Ole Opry out of Nashville, Tennessee, a radio show listened to at the time by almost everyone.

In crowded juke joints throughout the Deep South, popular blues songs were sung by men like Charley Patton who accompanied themselves on acoustic guitars. In big cities such as

Memphis, stomping piano blues with a
jumping, boogie-woogie beat was what
audiences clamored to hear, particularly
in and around the houses of prostitution
near Beale Street. In certain parts of the
United States, even whites occasionally
bought this music and listened to it on
phonographs or, more rarely, heard black
artists on the radio.

Bessie Smith

Despite the hardships of the Great
Depression, music provided some
opportunity for a handful of African-
Americans. A black woman who had beauty, a soul-stirring voice,
some dancing skills, and the ability to move a crowd to tears or to
its feet could make it to the vaudeville or medicine show circuit and
perhaps become a minor celebrity. If she had extraordinary talent,
as did Smith, Waters and Alberta Hunter, she might get a recording
contract and become a blues queen, a genuine star among her
people.

Robert Johnson, too, wanted the life of a successful musician.
As author Peter Guralnick put it, "[Delta bluesmen such as] Muddy
Waters, Johnny Shines, Robert Lockwood, Howlin' Wolf, and
Robert Johnson were bright, imaginative young men who knew
what they didn't want, which was to pick cotton like their parents
or be stuck in a rural backwater where their music was a diversion
— but a diversion only — from backbreaking labor."

But Johnson never achieved fame or financial success in his
lifetime. He lived a brief, nomadic life that is difficult to trace. He
made 59 recordings at two Texas recording sessions in 1936 and in
1937, of which 42 have survived.[2] He died a mysterious death in
1938, at age 27. He was unknown to all except a handful of family

---

[2]According to music historian and Robert Johnson archivist Steve
LaVere, 59 recordings were originally shipped to New York from these
two sessions. Only 42 of these masters have been located.

members, lovers and friends. Relatively few blues fans actually saw him perform or heard one of his records. They sold so modestly, in fact, that they weren't issued again to the buying public for nearly 25 years. His biggest seller, "Terraplane Blues," sold a mere 5,000 copies.

After World War II, a wave of African-American musicians migrated from the South to big industrial cities like Chicago in the North. Using new electronically amplified instruments, like the guitar, they began creating a new sound, one with a distinctive hard-driving, pulsing rhythm that could easily cut through the din of a crowded nightclub.

During the folk music boom of the 1950s and early 1960s, blues to many white folk purists meant acoustic guitars and vocal recordings of artists such as Leadbelly (real name Huddie Ledbetter), who transformed old and familiar story-songs such as "John Henry" into powerful artistic statements. As the civil rights movement began to gain acceptance among liberal-minded white college students, protest and work songs representing the views of American blacks enjoyed a brief but important vogue and inspired major folk artists such as Bob Dylan, who recorded his own idiosyncratic music that was often categorized as blues.

A hip-wiggling poor white boy from Memphis named Elvis Presley, who undoubtedly listened to blues while walking through the black part of town on Beale Street, recorded in 1954 a version of bluesman Arthur "Big Boy" Crudup's "That's All Right" at a tiny Memphis recording studio called Sun Records. This song — a blues tune with a fast, hard beat — ignited a music revolution that came to be known as rock 'n' roll. Although it is hard to believe today, Elvis' version of "That's All Right" sounded so much like a black singer to white listeners that disk jockey Dewey Phillips purposely asked Elvis on his radio show what Memphis high school he attended to clue in his audience that Elvis was white.

Rock 'n' roll music became popular around the world. It also stimulated a cross-pollination of musical genres and collaborations between artists of all colors and nationalities. Only a decade after

Elvis strummed his first chord, a group of young art school students in England discovered blues on imported American records and set out to duplicate the plaintive, primal power of this otherworldly music for their own loyal audiences. British groups such as the Rolling Stones, the Yardbirds and the Animals sent a highly amplified hybrid of blues and rock 'n' roll back across the Atlantic Ocean to an American youth market that had heard nothing like it before. A legion of white guitar players began to replicate the blues licks of British artists such as Eric Clapton, Keith Richards, and Jeff Beck, often unaware that these artists learned much of their technique from African -American blues masters.

It wasn't long, however, before these young guitarists and blues fans rediscovered the blues in their own backyards. Bluesmen such as B. B. King, Albert King, Muddy Waters and Howlin' Wolf found themselves playing for whites at stadiums, coliseums and rock emporiums such as The Fillmore East instead of the nightclubs and lounges where they had risen to blues prominence in the black community. Going from the so-called chitlin' circuit to the concert circuit was a big change for the bluesmen, who had hustled their whole lives to keep a few dollars in their pockets.

Clapton, a young London guitar player at the time, had left the popular band the Yardbirds because they were making pop hits for teenagers rather than playing the blues he loved. He then joined a blues group led by John Mayall. Mayall believed Clapton was perhaps the finest blues guitarist in England and set out to prove it. Clapton had already discovered the album *Robert Johnson: King of the Delta Blues Singers*, which had been released in 1961 and contained 16 of Johnson's recordings. Clapton became entranced with the lonesome moans and cries of this mysterious bluesman.

Eric Clapton recorded his first Robert Johnson song, "Ramblin' On My Mind," with John Mayall's group, the Bluesbreakers. It was the only slow, country blues song on the album, which was titled *John Mayall's Bluesbreakers with Eric Clapton*, and was a startling change of pace from the fire-breathing virtuosity of Clapton's searing and loud guitar work on the rest of the tracks.

When Clapton left the Bluesbreakers for a new group called Cream and cut another Robert Johnson tune, "Crossroads" (the title was abbreviated from "Cross Road Blues"), the legend of Robert Johnson began to spread worldwide. "Crossroads" not only outsold all of Robert Johnson's recordings put together, but in all likelihood outsold the entire output of Delta blues released on record prior to World War II. Eric Clapton spoke often of the inspiration he got from Robert Johnson.

Robert Johnson's music also impacted the self-described "World's Greatest Rock 'n' Roll Band" — the Rolling Stones. In the wake of the Beatles' success in America in 1964, scores of British bands were given recording contracts and hyped as the next big thing. Most of these groups geared their songs, usually sweet and catchy pop fluff, to the teen market. The Rolling Stones, however, managed to carve a unique niche for themselves as the bad boys of rock 'n' roll. Despite this image, the Rolling Stones were hard-working rhythm-and-blues diehards who often recorded brilliant versions of obscure blues songs.

As a result of the success of Eric Clapton and his version of "Crossroads," the Rolling Stones and many other artists became interested in recording other Robert Johnson tunes. After the release of "Crossroads," bootleg copies of the unreleased songs of Robert Johnson began to circulate among some of the privileged, well-connected blues connoisseurs, such as Mick Jagger and Keith Richards. Before the public had ever heard the Robert Johnson version of the song (unless they were collectors of rare, vintage 78s), the Rolling Stones recorded "Love In Vain," abbreviated from the title "Love In Vain Blues," for their hit album *Let It Bleed* in 1969. That same year, after a sabbatical from the road for an extended period, the Stones began a highly publicized tour of the United States. They prominently featured "Love In Vain" in their set, and a live version was recorded and released on another hit album, *Get Yer Ya-Ya's Out*.

When exposure to the music of Robert Johnson seemed to be reaching a peak, Columbia Records released another album containing 16 more Johnson recordings on *King of the Delta Blues Singers, Vol. II* in 1970.[3] "Love In Vain" was finally heard as recorded by its originator. The dam burst and Robert Johnson soon became an American icon, a figure known as much for his legend as his music. His name would become synonymous with Delta blues. Yet the man himself would remain shrouded in mystery.

---

[3]The album contained two tracks repeated from the first LP, "Rambling On My Mind" and "Preaching Blues."

The Life of
Robert Johnson

CHAPTER 1

THE EARLY YEARS

Robert Leroy Johnson was born in Hazlehurst, Miss., on May 8, 1911, or thereabouts.[4] Like many "facts" about Robert Johnson, there is dispute and debate among the experts. No birth certificate is known to exist. According to some sources, birth certificates were not required in Mississippi until 1912. The 1911 date is the one that is generally agreed upon by the most reputable researchers.

To further confuse matters, however, it isn't certain what name would have been given to Robert Johnson if such a document had ever been filed in the rural backwater of Hazlehurst in the first place. According to several acquaintances of Johnson who were interviewed years later, Johnson went by the name Robert Spencer as a boy in school. He changed his name to Robert Johnson as a teenager when he discovered the family secret — that he was an "outside child." He was born out of wedlock, his biological father a different man from either of the men who, during sequential periods of his life, had raised him.

Julia Majors Dodds, Robert's mother, had 10 children before Robert was born. Julia had married a successful wicker furniture

---

[4]Technically, Hazlehurst falls outside the parameters of what, geographically, constitutes the Mississippi Delta. Mississippians, particularly those descendents of the landed gentry class of Delta plantation owners, are sticklers for such things. That said, Robert Johnson spent the majority of his life in and around the Mississippi and Arkansas sides of the Delta.

maker and landowner, Charles Dodds, in 1889, and the family apparently lived reasonably well as the Dodds family grew larger year by year. According to several blues historians, Dodds was forced to leave Hazlehurst around 1909 after two prominent white landowner neighbors, the Marchetti brothers, threatened to have him lynched. According to one story, he escaped a mob by disguising himself as a woman and heading to Memphis, a city big enough and far enough from Hazlehurst to safely hide in. To make sure he wouldn't easily be found, he changed his name from Charles Dodds to C.D. (Charles Dodds) Spencer.

Julia stayed behind in Hazlehurst, and when it was safe began to relocate her children one by one to live in Memphis with their father. While living apart from her husband, Julia became acquainted with a farmhand named Noah Johnson, with whom she began an affair. Robert was born to the couple out of wedlock during this time. As Noah moved from job to job and plantation to plantation as a sharecropper, Julia left Hazlehurst, consigning herself and her two youngest children to a migrant labor agent for a few years.

News that his wife was living with another man and had a child by him apparently did not upset Charles Dodds Spencer. He had acquired a mistress named Serena and had fathered two children with her. The two women actually lived for a short time together with Spencer, but eventually Julia abandoned both the marriage and the boy. Surprisingly, considering the circumstances, Spencer took Robert in and even gave the child his new last name.

During childhood, Robert became acquainted with the guitar through his older half-brother, Charles Leroy, who later became known as a pianist. It isn't known how much experience Robert had playing the guitar during this time, but almost all of Robert's contemporaries agree that when he first began to perform years later his guitar-playing skills were amateurish at best. Several people who were acquainted with the young Robert Johnson recalled in interviews years later that the first instruments he played were the diddley bow and Jew's harp. The diddley bow was a homemade folk instrument played by countless African-American children throughout the Delta in the pre-War years. It is typically a one-string instrument made by unraveling the wire from a broomstick and stringing the wire between two nails that are spaced two to three feet apart. Some players made the base platform out of a section of a two-by-four or other wood. Others simply used the side of a house, nailing the nails and stringing the wire on any good spot they could find. To raise the string up from its base so it could be plucked, a small section of wood just a bit taller than the nails was placed under the string at one end.

A young boy plays a diddley bow nailed to the side of a sharecropper's shack in rural Mississippi circa 1930s.

The diddley bow was then played by plucking the string with a handmade pick and sliding a bottle, piece of pipe, knife edge or other smooth object over the string to vary the pitch. A good diddley-bow player can get an astonishing array of sounds and notes out of this primitive instrument. Some historians claim that the diddley bow is a variation of the African *umakweyana*, played by the women of Swaziland. Other one-stringed instruments from the Ivory Coast of West Africa, where the majority of slaves were from, no doubt also influenced the design of the diddley bow.

Hawaiian music became an entertainment fad in America in the 1920s and popularized a form of guitar playing now routinely described, when applied to blues, as slide guitar. In this style of playing, a guitar is tuned to a chord and a metal or glass object is used to slide up and down the strings to vary the pitch. It is reasonable to draw a connection between Hawaiian slide playing on the lap steel guitar and the slide style of the diddley bow.

Diddley-bow playing served as a musical foundation for Robert Johnson and several other Delta blues musicians who refined and developed the technique for the guitar. Hawaiian guitar has lost much of its popularity, but blues slide playing is today heard everywhere, in movie soundtracks, car commercials and even in the church. Johnson influenced several generations of guitar players with his remarkable virtuosity on slide guitar. They include Keith Richards, who claimed that when he heard Johnson's recordings for the first time he thought he was hearing two guitar players instead of one.

Hawaiian steel guitar playing was popular in the 1920s and 1930s and influenced slide guitar styles of Delta bluesmen. Pictured here is Joseph Kekuku, who was a master steel guitarist and revered by several generations of Hawaiian players.

In addition to the diddley bow and Jew's harp, Robert learned to play the harmonica, a mainstay of the Delta blues style. Although Johnson never played the harmonica on any of his recordings, bluesman Johnny Shines among others claimed that Johnson was quite accomplished on the instrument. The diddley bow and harmonica undoubtedly helped Johnson formulate the many voicings he adapted for his unique guitar style. Even the droning twang of the Jew's harp can be identified in some of the walking bass notes Johnson played on the heavy top strings of his guitar.[5]

---

[5]Johnson played these notes with a thumb pick which gives the bass strings a harder snap than the bare thumb. The thumb pick can be seen on Johnson's thumb in the Hooks Brothers studio portrait.

Piano music also influenced Johnson's style. It could be heard in the black section of Memphis, in the blues joints on Beale Street and in the parlors of the nearby brothels. Critics have noted that Johnson transposed many piano phrasings to the guitar. A close listen to Johnson's articulate technique reveals an enviable inventiveness, and many of his fillips and turnarounds have "piano" stamped all over them.

While Johnson was living in Memphis with his stepfather from about 1914 to 1918, his mother moved to the area around Robinsonville, Miss., and married a field hand named Willie "Dusty" Willis. Robert would not see his mother again for several years, until he and his sister Carrie came upon her by accident in Memphis. As Carrie told the story, while walking down Front Street in Memphis one day, she pointed and shouted, "That's Mama." This chance encounter reunited Robert with his mother, who took him back to Robinsonville to live with her and his new stepfather. But for young Robert, it was not to be a happy time, and music would increasingly become his escape from a fractured home life and the oppressive world of the Mississippi cotton plantation.

JOHNSON AS A
YOUNG MAN

He was lazy and good for nothing. That was the verdict Dusty Willis rendered about his new stepson, Robert. By all accounts Dusty Willis was a strict, no-nonsense, hard-nosed field laborer. When he was walking somewhere, he did so with such haste that he kicked up the dust at his feet, thus the nickname Dusty. Working the cotton fields was exhausting, mind-numbing work that paid barely enough to put food in the mouths of his children. To have a layabout stepson slouching around the house with nothing better to do than daydream and slip off at night was too much for the stern, single-minded Dusty Willis.

To no one's surprise, the two did not get along. Johnson worked the cotton fields as little as possible and apparently took a lot of verbal and physical abuse from his stepfather as a result. It was at this point in his life that Johnson for the first time adopted the surname of his biological father, Noah Johnson. He changed his last name possibly as an affront to his strict stepfather and, further, to declare himself a man.

Robinsonville, Miss., was home to the huge Leatherman plantation and like the vast feudal estates of the Middle Ages in England, within the larger society were several smaller societies. Because cotton was such an untrustworthy commodity to farm — one never knew if it would be a bumper crop year or a disaster — many field workers in the Delta made and sold moonshine, illegal corn whiskey.

Robinsonville was located in a dry county. That, of course, never stopped the flow of alcohol. Corn whiskey was a fact of life in those times, and it put money in the pockets of many people who would otherwise have been destitute. There was no upside to this scenario. Moonshine created the same social ills that legally obtained liquor does today. As we shall see later, bad moonshine could be lethal as well.

Juke joints were the logical places to sell and drink corn whiskey, and on Saturday nights business boomed. Wherever people gather to drink there is bound to be some type of entertainment, usually lively music. These were Johnson's training grounds as he grew into a young man.

Although records indicate that Johnson spent at least part of his youth at the Indian Creek School in Tunica, it isn't known how much schooling he had or how far he went. He also had a "lazy eye," which may have been a birth defect. It caused one eye to appear smaller than the other and more closed (see cover of this book). Some have suggested that Johnson may have had a cataract; others remember him having trouble in school from bad eyesight in the one eye. It is believed, though, that Johnson could read and write (some cite as evidence a death note he allegedly wrote), and the fluid penmanship apparent in his signatures on his marriage certificates suggests that he completed elementary school at a minimum. During the Great Depression few black children were encouraged to get a quality education or advance beyond the sixth or seventh grade. Most were put to work in the fields to help support their families.

Dusty Willis had tried and failed to get Johnson to do much work around the plantation. Perhaps as punishment, he forbade Johnson from hanging around the juke joints, which held a special lure and fascination for Johnson and most of the other local boys. As Son House tells it in Peter Guralnick's book: "His mother and stepfather didn't like for him to go out to those Saturday night balls because the guys were so rough. He didn't care anything about working in the fields, and his father was so tight on him about slipping out and coming where we were, so he just got the idea he'd run away from home." Where he may have run to is not clear. But the attraction of the musician's life must have taken hold as he watched famous bluesmen such as Charley Patton, Son House, Willie Brown and others play the local joints as well as the house rent parties, fish fries and other Saturday night "balls."

At the age of 18, Johnson fell in love and married a local girl, Virginia Travis, who was still in her early teens. Little is known about her. In April 1930, one year after their marriage, Virginia died giving birth and the child died as well. No one knows the impact of this tragedy on the young Johnson, although childbirth deaths were far from uncommon in those times. Some have suggested that the death of his wife brought down a psychological black curtain for Johnson — that this was the real crossroads in his life. Robert may have been away from home when Virginia went into labor and died. In addition to the grief he suffered, his wife's family blamed him for abandoning Virginia in her time of need.

Whatever the truth, Johnson was never again rooted in any one place. He wandered from town to town and from woman to woman, with only whiskey and music as his constant companions. The songs he was soon to write were almost always about a relationship with a woman and the fear of losing someone you love.

CHAPTER 3

THE WALKING MUSICIAN YEARS

A fter the death of his wife and child, Johnson knew he could not go back home to live with his mother and demanding stepfather and work on a cotton plantation. He had been drawn to the music and the lifestyle of the blues players who worked at the joints and roadhouses for a few dollars and all the corn whiskey they could drink. Most of these men dressed sharp, acted cool and stole the hearts of all the women they could handle. To Johnson and others, the life of a walking musician — those players who traveled from town to town earning a dollar here and there — was far preferable to the harsh life of sharecropping.

Johnson had already taught himself to play the diddley bow and Jew's harp, two crude but helpful instruments for a beginning bluesman. According to a childhood friend, Israel "Wink" Clark, Johnson had even modified his diddley bow to more closely resemble a guitar. "He had three nails and three strands of wire nailed up on the east side of his house and put him a bottle in there to keep the strings from layin' flat, to tighten 'em like for tunin', and that's what he started with. And that's just how he started playin' music on that bottle and three strands of wire."

Johnson had graduated to the harmonica, gotten good at that, and moved on to the guitar, which at first proved to be more difficult for him. He probably started off with a Stella guitar, an inexpensive brand popular among blues musicians. Just as when he was younger, Johnson liked to go to the juke joints to listen to other musicians, such as Son House. It wasn't long before Johnson began asking for permission to play with the professionals. As Son House told the story to writer/musician John Fahey:

> So Robert, he would be standing around, and he would listen, too, and he got the idea that he'd like to play. So he started from that and everywhere that he'd get to hear us playing for a Saturday night ball, he would come and be there …
>
> So when we'd get to a rest period or something, we'd set the guitars up and go out — it would be hot in the summertime, so we'd go out and get in the cool — cool off some. While we're out, Robert, he'd get the guitar and go to bamming with it, you know? Just keeping noise, and the people didn't like that. They'd come and tell us, "Why don't you or Willie go in there and stop that boy? He's driving everybody nuts … "
>
> But as quick as we're out of there again, and get to laughing and talking and drinking, here we'd hear the guitar again, making all kinds of tunes: BLOO-WAH, BOOM-WAH — a dog wouldn't want to hear it!

Son House then claimed that the next time he heard Johnson perform an incredible change had taken place.

> I said, "Look who's coming in the door, got a guitar on his back."
>
> [Willie Brown] said, "Yeah, no kidding." He said, "Oh, that's Little Robert."
>
> I said, "Yeah, that's him." I said, "Don't say nothing."
>
> And he wiggled through the crowd, until he got over to where we was. I said, "Boy, now where you going with that thing? T'annoy somebody else to death again?"
>
> He say, "I'll tell you what, too." He say, "This your rest time?"
>
> I say, "Well, we can make it our rest time. What you want to do, annoy the folks?"
>
> He say, "No, just let me—give me a try."
>
> I say, "Well, OK." I winked at Willie. So me and Willie got up, and I gave him my seat. He set down. And that boy got

started off playing ... and when he got through, all our mouths were standing open. All! He was gone!

In the two years time that Robert was gone away from the Robinsonville area, he traveled by hitching rides ("hoboing") on freight trains. During the years of the Great Depression, thousands of people, many of them men who were unemployed and looking for seasonal labor, rode the rails. Riding inside a boxcar in the summer heat could be suffocating and riding in the dead of winter freezing. The trains were often dirty, dusty, unsanitary and dangerous. Railroad security officers ("railroad bulls") frequently brutalized the illegal train riders, especially if they were black.

As hazardous as hoboing could be, many found it an acceptable way of life and liked the freedom it afforded to be able to pick up and move farther down the line whenever the itch to travel was too great to resist. Johnson, with his restless ways, found freight trains the ideal mode of transportation. He didn't have to pay, and if he watched his back he could travel in relative peace without anyone ordering him to do anything, which was a far cry from the regimentation of life on the plantation. Traveling with only his guitar and necessary clothes, he found he could earn a little money here and there playing during market day around town squares or by finding the juke joints and roadhouses in the black parts of town that needed some entertainment. It wasn't uncommon for a juke joint to book two or three different acts on Saturday nights, enough to keep the people coming until the wee hours, drinking as much liquor as they could hold.

Although many of the stories about Johnson from his contemporaries offer contradictory information, a portrait of the man still emerges from the more consistent elements. Johnson was small of stature, round-shouldered, and somewhat frail, not particularly possessed of a fighting spirit unless liquor took hold of him. He was quiet and introspective by nature and comfortable enough within his own skin to be alone for long stretches of time. On train trips with other musicians such as Johnny Shines, whom he would meet some years later in Helena, Ark., he could sit and stare into the passing scenery without speaking a word for hours on end. He was impulsive about moving on when he felt it was time and didn't particularly care one way or the other if his friends were ready to go with him or not. "Robert was a strange dude," said bluesman Robert Jr. Lockwood. "I guess you could say he was a loner and a drifter."

Several of his acquaintances mentioned a peculiar habit of Johnson's: When he was ready to leave a town, a party, a juke joint or gathering of any kind, he would simply disappear. Many people would not notice he was gone until long after the fact.

Johnson also at this point in his life never seemed to be satisfied with one woman. Although reserved most of the time, Johnson was a notorious flirt, and he wasn't concerned whether they were attached or not — married or single didn't matter to him as long as they were available. When he was drinking, according to the recollections of several bluesmen who knew him, no woman was off limits. Not surprisingly, he got in a number of fights and scrapes that he wasn't capable of backing up with his own fists. The dirty work was usually left to others to settle. As Johnny Shines said in one interview:

> Sometimes I'd get the worst of something Robert started ... He couldn't punch hisself out of a wet paper sack. I've seen many people with the same build that he had that were much more capable of taking care of themselves than he was. He wasn't a scrapper or a fighter, but he tried, and he'd get the hell beat out of *you* if you didn't watch out. 'Cause he'd jump on a gang of guys just as quick as he would one, and if you went to defend him, why, naturally you'd get it.

"Women, to Robert, were like motel or hotel rooms," Shines added in another interview. "Even if he used them repeatedly he left them where he found them ... He preferred older women in their thirties over the younger ones, because the older ones would pay his way."

Johnson was not above scouting out potential "sugar mamas" in the towns he played, and these women, often abandoned, lonely, plain-looking and love-starved, were easy pickings for a slim, young dandy like Johnson. A succession of women kept Johnson fed, clothed and romantically satisfied during some very lean times, and although this sounds like Johnson took unfair advantage of practically every woman he met, few of his lovers interviewed years later spoke negatively about their relationships with him.

Only a few years after the death of his first wife, Johnson met and married another woman, Calletta "Callie" Craft, who seemed to be a perfect blueprint for the new type of woman Johnson wanted. She was plain-looking, more than 10 years older than Johnson, large and heavyset, and willing to spend her money and time any way her new husband saw fit. She had been married and divorced twice before she met Johnson and had three children. According to researcher Stephen LaVere, Callie Craft so doted on "Little Robert" that she served him breakfast in bed. Curiously, the marriage, at Johnson's request, was kept secret from all but a handful of people. Why? Doubtless because Johnson had no intention of settling down with one woman and didn't want the trappings of marriage, such as a gold wedding band around his finger, to interfere with his indiscretions.

They were wed in 1931 and moved to the Clarksdale, Miss., area about two years later. In photographs Callie Craft seems robust and healthy, but looks can be deceiving. She fell on ill health and hard times soon after moving to Clarksdale. Johnson abandoned her there. She died soon after, in 1934. It isn't known if Johnson cared one way or the other about his second wife's death.

Johnson's rambling ways left many friends and lovers behind and saw only one positive outcome — his exposure to a wide cross-section of blues players and audiences had helped mold him into an expert musician and entertainer. He had spent time around his birthplace of Hazlehurst learning from an older mentor named Ike Zinermon. He also had seen and on occasion performed with some

Sonny Boy Williamson II (standing) and band performing on the *King Biscuit Time* radio show in Helena, Ark., in 1944. (Photograph courtesy of the Gladin Collection, Southern Media Archives, University of Mississippi Libraries)

of the most venerated bluesmen of the era including Son House, Tommy Johnson, Willie Brown, Charley Patton, Howlin' Wolf, Honeyboy Edwards, Lonnie Johnson, Aleck "Rice" Miller (also known as Sonny Boy Williamson II) and a host of others.

As he perfected his craft, Robert Johnson began to write his own songs, keeping the words and notes to himself in a tiny notebook. Johnson had such an acute ear for music that his peers claimed he could hear a song once on a radio or jukebox and play it practically note for note on the guitar afterward. This talent would earn him a lot of coins when he played for crowds around town courthouses, train depots and the like.

Sometime in the mid-1930s Johnson began to travel more on the Arkansas side of the great alluvial plain referred to as the Delta. Helena, Ark., which is located just across the Mississippi River from the greater Clarksdale, Miss., area became a rendezvous point for many blues musicians and was later the home of the popular *King Biscuit Time* radio show, which featured live performances by bluesmen, including Sonny Boy. It was around Helena that Johnson met and befriended Johnny Shines, the most eloquent and poetic bluesman among Johnson's friends.

Shines, who died in 1992, was one of the most dependable and accurate sources for anecdotes on Johnson. From the many interviews he gave, blues researchers have concluded that Shines felt Johnson was an artist of immense talent who influenced practically all the blues that came afterwards. Shines claimed that the complex chord structures in some of Johnson's songs had an immediate impact on blues players at the time and predicted that if Johnson had lived, he may have turned more to jazz in his playing. "I thought Robert was about the greatest guitar player I'd ever heard," Shines told one interviewer. "The things he was doing was things that I'd never heard nobody else do, and I wanted to learn it. Robert changed everything, what you might say."

Shines traveled with Johnson not only in the South, but to big cities in the North such as Chicago and St. Louis. Shines was always impressed by the way Johnson would carefully roll up his trousers and lay out his suit jacket so that even after riding the rails for days at a time he could simply shake his clothes out and look fresh-pressed and clean when he entered a new town.

In spite of their friendship and days spent together traveling, Shines never felt he truly got inside the mind of his friend. In later years Johnny Shines would describe Johnson as a man who was essentially unknowable, who kept his private thoughts private. Shines said that it was only years after the fact that he knew anything at all of Johnson's background — where he was from, who his people were, whether or not he had ever been married. What he saw in Johnson was a man almost wholly preoccupied with his music whose other interests happened also to be his worst vices: whiskey and women.

In less than five years Robert Johnson had achieved his dream. He was a walking musician. Other seasoned musicians not only respected him but were often in awe of him and his abilities. He could attract a crowd in just about any new town he came to and make money just by performing on street corners, playing almost any song called out to him, whether a cowboy tune such as "Tumbling Tumbleweeds" or a Tin Pan Alley pop staple such as "My Blue Heaven." According to Shines, Johnson even had a talent for playing polkas. He left audiences in juke joints all over the South wanting more of his blues and clamoring for some of the songs he had written himself, such as "Terraplane Blues," which capitalized on the popularity of the stylish, streamlined Hudson Terraplane automobile. Johnson had women wherever he went and even once had a female midget running his errands for him while he lodged at the Hunt Hotel in West Memphis, Ark.

Life, even during the depths of the Great Depression, was better than good for this traveling bluesman. There was only one more major step he needed to make.

CHAPTER 4

THE RECORDING YEARS

H.C. Speir's music store in Jackson, Miss., was a pulsing hub of activity on Saturdays for the local black population. Speir, who was white, had purposely located his store on North Farish Street and later West Capitol Street in the heart of the black business district to capitalize on a market neglected by most other white business owners. During the 1920s, Speir's store did an impressive business selling musical instruments, phonograph players and 78 rpm phonograph records. On good days he could sell 600 or more records. Each cost from 35 cents for budget-label recordings up to 75 cents for premium big-label recordings — a considerable sum of money for that time — and virtually every record sold featured a black singer or musician.

Speir had diversified business interests. One was scouting black talent for major record companies, including Victor, Okeh, Paramount and Columbia. Because so many musicians were customers at his music store, he had an almost endless stream of talent to choose from. He was paid a basic finder's fee when an artist was signed to a record

H. C. Speir during his retirement years
(Photo courtesy of the Speir family)

label, and he usually recorded a few demonstration songs when he felt an unknown artist merited a record company's attention. Speir owned one of the very few audition recording machines in the South and installed it in a makeshift studio upstairs in his store. He discovered some of the Mississippi Delta's most important blues artists, including Charley Patton, Bo Carter, Skip James, the Mississippi Sheiks and Tommy Johnson. He auditioned countless singers and musicians from the 1920s up until the 1940s.

In 1936, a sharply dressed Robert Johnson visited Speir's store. Johnson auditioned and impressed the talent scout enough that he apparently recorded at least one demo with him, although it has never been found. Speir recommended mostly artists with original material, so it's fair to assume that Johnson's original songs, such as "Terraplane Blues," convinced him of Johnson's commercial potential. Speir's rule of thumb was that an artist had to have at least four good originals to be worthy of recording.

Ernie Oertle, a regional salesman for the American Record Corporation (known as ARC), frequently called on Speir, who was an important client because of the high volume of ARC records Speir sold in his store. Speir forwarded contact information for Johnson to Oertle. On the strength of Speir's recommendation and possibly a demo acetate he had recorded of Johnson in his store, Oertle located Johnson and made arrangements to have him travel to San Antonio, Texas, in late November 1936 to make his first recordings.

San Antonio was a hotbed of recording talent in those years and was home to a variety of music styles. Cowboy vocal groups, such as the Chuck Wagon Gang, Mexican mariachi bands, hillbilly trios, and even African-American blues singers all found their way to this multi-cultural South Texas city. Don Law, a record producer born in London, was in charge of the Dallas branch of ARC. He had set up a makeshift studio in the Gunter Hotel in San Antonio on behalf of Art Satherly, who was in charge of production for ARC. Johnson was sent to Law and Satherly in the hope of making a few saleable records for the "race" market.

Johnson could not have been in more competent company. Law already had a reputation for letting "an artist be an artist." He had produced hits with Bob Wills and Al Dexter and was well liked and regarded by almost all who worked with him. In later years, he was to head up Columbia Records' country and western division, where he was responsible for cross-over hits by Johnny Cash, Marty Robbins, Lefty Frizzell and Johnny Horton — all major country artists. (Art Satherly also became a well-known executive for Columbia.) In 2001, Law was posthumously elected to the Country Music Hall of Fame.

By 1936 Law already had substantial experience with dozens of marquee-name performers, but years later he still vividly recalled his sessions with the then unknown Johnson. In talks and correspondence with Frank Driggs, who in 1961 wrote the liner notes for the *Robert Johnson: King of the Delta Blues Singers* album, he told several fanciful stories that have become pillars of the Robert Johnson legend. Law in many ways could be considered a trained observer and had expertise working with all types of performers, but his stories of Johnson still have scholars quarreling and scratching their heads.

Law's first impression of Robert Johnson was that he was a totally inexperienced blues singer straight out of the cotton patch. He was struck by Johnson's shyness and seeming lack of confidence. To Law, it seemed as if Johnson was a country bumpkin visiting the big city for the first time in his life. Of course he couldn't have been more wrong. By the time of Johnson's death in 1938, his travels had taken him far — to New York, St. Louis, Chicago, Detroit, even Canada. He was a practiced, seasoned professional who had performed in hundreds of venues and later even performed on radio. His crisp, well-pressed appearance to most people would have suggested a far more worldly man than Law took him for.

One of the oddest anecdotes Law later told was of Robert Johnson turning his back on him and the others in the room while he was being recorded. Theories have proliferated about why

Johnson did this. Law felt Johnson was so shy about his singing and playing that he couldn't stand to look anyone in the eye. He was "suffering from a bad case of stage fright," according to Law. However, this explanation is at odds with nearly every eyewitness account of Johnson's juke-joint and street-corner performances. According to those other firsthand reports, Johnson was a charismatic, crowd-pleasing professional.

Johnny Shines said Johnson didn't particularly like to practice his guitar in front of others and zealously guarded his playing techniques. But since Johnson was a very public performer, whose technique was right there for everyone to see, Shines' normally dependable memory might need to be called into question.

A more recent explanation is that Johnson was "corner-loading" to improve the acoustics of his sound. Corner-loading is somewhat like singing in the shower to get that reverb bounce off the tiles that makes an otherwise weak voice sound pretty grand. Playing and singing into a corner can approximate that kind of acoustic reverberation that appeals so much to the ear.

There are a lot of holes in this argument, however. This assumes that Johnson had experimented with his acoustics, but almost no one recalls him ever practicing his guitar much less finagling with the sound. It also assumes that Johnson was acquainted with the engineering science of electronic sound recording and the intricacies of microphone placement. Of course there is no evidence that he had any kind of working knowledge of the medium. No, he was new to it all.

A far simpler and more plausible reason is that Johnson turned away from the others to avoid distraction — the reality of being placed in front of a microphone in a recording studio gives even veteran performers attacks of the nerves — and better concentrate on what he was doing. Undoubtedly, he did not want to blow it. As Elijah Wald has written, this was Johnson's make-or-break moment. Had he botched take after expensive take he probably would have been shown the door. Other musicians were waiting their turn at the studio and during the Great Depression no one had the luxury of messing up. Johnson was a professional and he simply went to work and got the job done. More than 70 years after that first recording session in San Antonio, people are still passionate about the songs he put down.

To cut a record in those days was no easy task. Buddy Merrill, a legendary electric guitarist and pioneer of multi-track recording, had this to say about his early experiences with acetate recording:

> In 1954, I decided to venture into the realm of multiple recording with a 2-speed disc cutter and a monaural tape recorder. These machines were not of professional quality but they served well enough for my experiments. The biggest of several problems that I encountered was with the cutting stylus and the acetates. Sometimes, the acetates were imperfect and would not cut properly, and [there were] fine threads that came from the disc while the cutter was recording. These threads had to be brushed toward the center of the disk to prevent the cutter from running into them; otherwise, the cutting stylus would derail and jump from the disc creating a flawed and unusable recording.
>
> I enlisted help from my younger brother to remove the threads with a fine brush. Multi track recording took so much time using this method, the brushing became a tedious task my brother disliked. The recordings made on these machines were noisy and the wow created by the disc turntable was noticeable.

Each acetate was a big, clunky piece of lacquer-coated flat metal that was heavy, expensive, cumbersome and a pain to store. Standard recording procedure was to save only the two best takes: the better version was the one that would be used to press the shellac records later sold in stores and played on jukeboxes. If Johnson suffered from stage fright as Don Law recalled, it never surfaced in any noticeable way in any on the 42 surviving recordings. Johnson was surprisingly consistent from track to track.

Don Law told two other often-repeated stories about Johnson's first days in San Antonio. While dining with his wife one night at a restaurant in town, Law was summoned to the phone. It was the San Antonio police calling from the city jail. Johnson had been arrested for vagrancy. Law reportedly left the restaurant to bail Johnson out.

Upon returning to the restaurant and resuming his meal, Law was called to the phone a second time. This time it was Johnson himself on the line. He explained to Law that he had been feeling mighty lonesome while in jail and had found himself a lady (a prostitute no doubt) with whom he wanted to spend some time. His problem: "She wants fifty cents and I lacks a nickel."

Whether these stories are true is debatable. Don Law's son recounts the stories in the documentary film *The Search for Robert Johnson*. They are irresistibly funny. They also seem to fit pretty well with what little is known of Johnson's lifestyle. Producer John Hammond later referred to the "tall tales" he had heard about Johnson.

On November 23, 26 and 27, Johnson recorded 16 songs in more than 32 takes at the makeshift studio at the Gunter Hotel. The songs were: "Kindhearted Woman Blues," "I Believe I'll Dust My Broom," "Sweet Home Chicago," "Rambling On My Mind," "When You Got A Good Friend," "Come On In My Kitchen," "Terraplane Blues," "Phonograph Blues," "32-20 Blues," "They're Red Hot," "Dead Shrimp Blues," "Cross Road Blues," "Walking Blues," "Last Fair Deal Gone Down," "Preaching Blues (Up Jumped the Devil)," and "If I Had Possession Over Judgment Day."[6]

It is virtually certain that Robert Johnson didn't leave Texas with more than $100 in his pocket for his 16 songs. Recording artists almost never commanded much more than that. "About seventy-five to a hundred dollars was all the money he ever got," Johnny Shines confirmed. However, $100 during the Great Depression in Robinsonville, Miss., was a substantial sum of money — enough for him to be worried about being robbed.

---

[6]More information about the recordings can be found in several of the books listed in the bibliography.

Shortly after his recording sessions in San Antonio, his biggest-selling record was released, "Terraplane Blues," which made Robert Johnson something of a minor celebrity in the parts of the South he was known to travel. Son House recalled, "Jesus, it was good. We all admired it. Said, 'That boy is really going places.'" Others recalled the pride Johnson felt toward his records and the recording sessions for ARC. He often took copies of his records to the houses of friends and lovers to play for them. "Nearly every time I came upon Robert he'd be telling me about some new recording session," Johnny Shines recalled. "He'd tell me about things I'd never seen like 'start lights' and 'stop lights' used in recording."

Johnson occasionally drew a crowd on street corners with impromptu performances of "Terraplane Blues" and undoubtedly pocketed a few extra dollars when the audience realized that he was the same man as the one on the record. Predictably, Johnson used his newfound celebrity to attract even more women. At this time he was living off and on with Estella Coleman, the mother of Robert Jr. Lockwood, and romancing Willie Mae Cross and countless other women he encountered.

According to blues historian Gayle Dean Wardlow, Johnson got into trouble with the law at least one more time in his life. He was thrown in jail for a night along with musician Willie Moore for making fun of the high sheriff of Robinsonville, Miss., in a song they were singing on a street corner. Johnson went by several different names during his walking musician years, partly because of scrapes with the law, but mostly because of scrapes with jealous boyfriends and husbands. He was known in different places as both R. L. and his earlier name Robert Spencer. These aliases made the work that much harder for the first round of Johnson researchers.

In early 1938, Johnson traveled through Detroit with Johnny Shines, Shines' cousin Calvin Frazier, a bluesman, and another cousin, Sampson Pittman. They performed together on the Elder

Moten Hour radio show. Unfortunately, no recording of the performance has been found.

The summer before, in June 1937, ARC and Don Law scheduled a second series of recording sessions for Johnson, this time in a warehouse in downtown Dallas. Accordingly, the warehouse was so hot that summer that the performers would often strip to their underwear to record. Blocks of ice were placed in washtubs with fans blowing over them to keep the sweltering heat somewhat under control.

At his first Dallas session, Johnson recorded three songs; perhaps the heat made recording more difficult that day. The following day, a Sunday, Johnson recorded a wealth of material: 10 songs done in more than 20 takes. Out of these sessions came some of Johnson's most haunting songs — "Stones In My Passway," "Hellhounds On My Trail," and "Me and the Devil Blues" — that would serve as kindling for the crossroads myth that caught fire years later.

Johnson continued his travels throughout the Delta of Mississippi and Arkansas and ventured north into New York City, St. Louis, Chicago, and, according to Johnny Shines, parts of America where few black men had ever been seen. Johnson could not have known it, but forces were at work that would forever change his legend as well as his life. Powerful, well-placed figures in the music industry had discovered the music of this obscure bluesman down in Mississippi and wanted to bring his talents out in the open to the world at large. Luck, however, has a way of running out when people least expect it. Some would say darker forces were at work on Johnson, that the hellhounds he described in his song had finally caught his scent.

CHAPTER 5

DEATH OF A RISING STAR

There are two things about Robert Johnson on which virtually all parties agree: He loved whiskey and women. It should come as no surprise, then, that one of the hallmarks of the Johnson legend, his mysterious death, should revolve around those two things.

The one indisputable fact about his death is that he did, in fact, die, most probably on August 16, 1938, as is now verified on an official State of Mississippi death certificate that was unearthed in 1968 by blues researcher Gayle Dean Wardlow. But many other things written or spoken about the circumstances of Johnson's death since his passing have been cloaked in lies, exaggerations, misperceptions, half-truths and myth.

The tale most often told about how Johnson met his fate is that he was poisoned by a jealous husband who put strychnine in his whiskey. As the story goes, Johnson was booked to play at a rural juke joint just outside Greenwood, Miss., that Honeyboy Edwards recalled was named Three Forks. Johnson apparently had struck up an ill-advised affair with the juke-joint operator's wife, which would certainly be in character with Johnson's reputation as a womanizer. The operator reportedly mixed strychnine into whiskey that Johnson subsequently drank.

While performing later that night, Johnson reputedly took ill and had to be taken to a rooming house in the Baptist Town section of Greenwood where he languished for several days, perhaps weeks, before succumbing to the poison. He was buried at the Little Zion Church Cemetery, although no one is *precisely* sure where. A death certificate was filed and later amended following an interview with the plantation owner. No cause of death is listed on the certificate — only the words "No Doctor."

Gayle Dean Wardlow's discovery of the death certificate in 1968, and the later publication of the reverse side of the document in 1996, delivered a jolt to the blues world. The document's reverse side, written by the LeFlore County Registrar, states the following:

> I talked with the white man on whose place this negro died and I also talked with a negro woman on the place. The plantation owner said this negro man, seemingly about 26 years old, came down from Tunica two or three weeks before he died to play a banjo at a negro dance given there on the plantation. He staid (sic) in the house with some of the negroes saying he wanted to pick cotton. The white man did not have a doctor for this negro as he had not worked for him. He was buried in a homemade coffin furnished by the County. The plantation owner said it was his opinion that the negro died of syphilis.

The notion that Johnson may have contracted and died of syphilis set tongues wagging and minds reeling. A few blues scholars still cling to this diagnosis. Others, however, have expressed indignation and outrage at a notion they find absurd. Blues authority David Evans, one of the most respected voices on all matters related to Delta bluesmen, has called this alleged cause of death "bigoted nonsense," and, indeed, there is no evidence whatsoever that Johnson ever contracted a sexual disease of any kind much less syphilis, which normally takes years to take a fatal toll. End stage syphilis typically can cause blindness, madness and other instantly identifiable symptoms, none of which would seem to apply to Johnson's known life.

One consequence of the plantation owner's claim of syphilis as the cause of death was that it released anyone of the responsibility

Johnson's death certificate (front). Note the words "No Doctor" written on the document.

of seriously investigating the death for foul play. It also may have been, as David Evans has suggested, a racist slap at young, itinerant black men, who according to the prevailing stereotype of the day, were so consumed by lust that an early death from

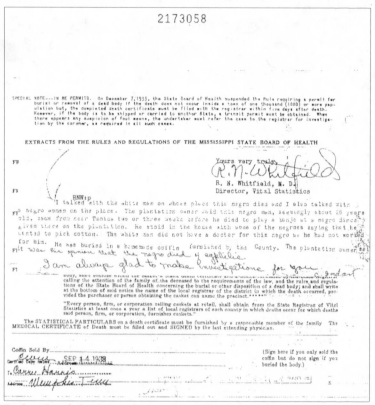

Back side of death certificate. This side contained a great deal more information, including the controversial opinion that Johnson's death had been due to "syphilis."

venereal disease would seem fitting and inevitable. By spreading the rumor that Johnson died of syphilis, the plantation owner also may have been sending a warning to the women in residence on his plantation to beware of transients and ne'er-do-well musicians.

The stereotype of black society being riddled with venereal disease came glaringly into light recently when a review of the medical records of Booker T. Washington, one of the 20th Century's most celebrated and learned African-American leaders, concluded that he died of high blood pressure, not "racial characteristics."

According to the Associated Press, the designation "racial characteristics" was "an often dismissive term [for] syphilis." The new findings by the University of Maryland pointed out that a blood test on Washington had ruled out syphilis as a cause of death, yet in 1915 the doctor in attendance wrote the damning words "racial characteristics" on the medical records, leaving historians to question the character and lifestyle of their subject.

With the syphilis diagnosis now discounted by most if not all of the experts on Johnson, historians are still left with the puzzle of the poisoning. Most blues scholars accept this version of events, although there are many quibbles over the details.

The problem with strychnine as the juke-joint operator's *modus operandi* is that, according to toxicologist Steve Nichols of the Shelby County Medical Examiner's Office in Memphis, Tenn., strychnine has a distinctively bitter taste and odor that would be difficult to disguise even in hard liquor. To be fatal, Nichols said, a significant amount would have to be consumed. A toxic dose also would cause death in a matter of hours, not days. And, according to the Centers for Disease Control, "the major identifying clinical features of strychnine poisoning through ingestion are severe, painful spasms of the neck, back, and limbs and convulsions with an intact sensorium. Symptoms might progress to coma. Tachycardia and hypertension are also common effects." No evidence has ever surfaced that Johnson suffered spasms, convulsions or a rapid heartbeat in his final days, or that he lapsed into a coma prior to death.

Is it possible that Johnson could have drank such a heavy quantity of bad-tasting liquor without becoming suspicious that something most foul was afoot? Of course, it is possible. More probable, however, is that Johnson either bought or was given some deadly moonshine — maybe on purpose, maybe not — the night he took sick. Moonshine, corn liquor made with any number of toxic ingredients including lead, killed far more Mississippi blacks in the pre-War era than strychnine-laced whiskey dispensed by jealous husbands.

Son House, the contemporary of Johnson who knew him well and performed with him during his walking musician days, once warned Johnson specifically about mixing bad liquor with bad women.

> You have to be careful, 'cause you mighty crazy about the girls. When you playing for these balls and these girls get full of that corn whiskey and snuff mixed together, and you be playing a good piece and they like it and call you, "Daddy, play it again, daddy," well, don't let it run you crazy. You liable to get killed.

Bad moonshine could explain why Sonny Boy Williamson and Honeyboy Edwards claimed that, before dying, Johnson had been observed "crawling around ... slobbering and going on and heaving up" (quote attributed to Honeyboy Edwards). For the rest of his life, the colorful and loquacious Sonny Boy Williamson would tell everyone that he observed Johnson crawling on all fours and barking like a dog shortly before he died, and that it was he who held Johnson as he drew his dying breath. As musician Levon Helm recalled of one such incident with Sonny Boy, "While we waited [in a barbecue joint], someone asked Sonny Boy whether he'd known Robert Johnson. '*Knew him?*' Sonny Boy asked incredulously. 'Boy, Robert Johnson *died in my arms!*'"

Johnson researchers, many of whom seem unwilling to part with the romantic notion of the bluesman being poisoned by a jealous husband, have modified the story to fit the fact that strychnine poisoning kills in hours instead of days. Several now claim that Johnson was indeed poisoned but did not die from it. Instead, he was in such a weakened state that he contracted a fatal case of pneumonia. Another rumor is that moth balls were mixed into Johnson's drink.[7]

---

[7] Another recent opinion offered by David Connell in the *BMJ* (*British Medical Journal*) is that Johnson may have died of Marfan's Syndrome, an inherited disease that affects connective tissues in the body.

Blues historian Mack McCormick, a man who figures prominently in the afterlife of Johnson, claims on camera in the documentary film *The Search for Robert Johnson* that he not only knew the name of the jealous husband who poisoned Johnson but that he had even gotten a confession of sorts from the man. McCormick, who has often been dismissed as a crackpot, comes across as the supreme authority in this film and seems entirely believable and convincing. Yet he refuses to name names and has shut off almost all communication on the subject of Robert Johnson, leaving us to wonder if there is any truth to his assertions. A lot of people believe him, a lot don't.

According to author Peter Guralnick, McCormick also claimed he had found two eyewitnesses to Johnson's murder. As Guralnick quotes him: "The accounts agreed substantially as to the motive, the circumstances, and in naming the person responsible for the murder. It had been a casual killing that no one took very seriously. In their eyes Robert Johnson was a visiting guitar player who got murdered."

Whispers have circulated for some time that the rumored murderer was last seen in the mid-1970s in Key West, Fla. This rumor, like all the other ones, is impossible to prove or disprove, and only adds more smoke and fog to the legend.

A note reportedly in Johnson's handwriting has surfaced in recent years that is said to have been from the house where Johnson died on the Star of the West plantation. The note reads: "Jesus of Nazareth, King of Jerusalem, I know that my Redeemer liveth and that He will call me from the Grave." This "evidence" is discussed rather prominently in the liner notes to the Johnson CD box set and is reproduced on the tombstone that was erected in 2002 at the Little Zion M.B. Church cemetery. Most of the sources consulted for this book, however, fail to even mention this information, a certain indicator that most researchers are unaware of it.

The sentiments expressed in the note, which is a sort of deathbed confession, fit almost too neatly into the myth of Johnson selling his soul to the devil. What better bookend to the myth than

Although three gravestones at different sites claim to hold the remains of Johnson — (left) Quito, Miss., (middle) Morgan City, Miss., (right) Greenwood, Miss. — the state of Mississippi, relying on eyewitness accounts, recognizes the third one, at Little Zion M.B. Church outside Greenwood. (Photos by Tom Graves)

for Johnson, in his last minutes on this earth, to ask Jesus for forgiveness for the mortal sin of selling his soul? The death note, which may or may not be in Johnson's handwriting (no one has stepped forward with conclusive evidence that it is) rings a bit false and convenient. A dying man, especially one who has been poisoned, isn't capable of doing much handwriting. Christian beliefs or not, Johnson was a bluesman who, from all reports, spoke very little of Jesus.[8]

One thing is for sure: No one knows definitively what killed Johnson. The only way to answer the dilemma would be to exhume his body and perform forensic tests on it. However, no one knows with any degree of certainty where he is buried.

Today three headstones mark the burial sites of Robert Leroy Johnson. One is in Quito, Miss., located next to the Payne Chapel not far from the juke joint where Johnson last played. A second site is two miles away, near Morgan City, Miss., at the Mount Zion Church. The third site, north of Greenwood, Miss., at the Little Zion M.B. Church was identified in 2000 and is now considered by the state as the most likely resting place of Johnson based on the

[8]The handwritten note was found among the papers and other effects belonging to Johnson's half-sister Carrie Thompson, who had possession of the two Johnson photographs.

testimony of an 86-year-old church member named Rosie Eskridge, who said her husband dug Johnson's grave and she witnessed the burial.

Perhaps the last word on the subject should go to an expert, Tony Burroughs, a renowned genealogist and the author of *Black Roots: A Beginner's Guide To Tracing the African-American Family Tree.* In a recent interview cited in *The* (Memphis) *Commercial Appeal*, he said, "No one record can prove a fact ... You have to take a multitude of records to prove a fact ... A death certificate is only one record." He added: "The best method [for researching a long-deceased African-American] is to weave together details found in oral histories, birth and death certificates, census records, baptism records, diaries, letters, family Bibles. Even then, there's only so much that can be known for sure." The Mississippi Delta has practically been turned upside down in the search for records of Johnson. So far only marriage application signatures, two photos, a death certificate, a disputed death note, a few scattered school documents and conflicting oral histories of the man exist.

The Afterlife of
Robert Johnson

CHAPTER 6

LEGEND OF
THE CROSSROADS

"Now if [Tommy Johnson] was living, he'd tell you," LeDell Johnson, Tommy's brother, told blues researcher David Evans in 1966. "He said the reason he knowed so much, said he sold hisself to the devil. I asked him how. He said,

> If you want to learn how to play anything you want to play and learn how to make songs yourself, you take your guitar and you go to where a road crosses that way, where a crossroads is. Get there, be sure to get there just a little 'fore 12:00 that night so you'll know you'll be there. You have your guitar and be playing a piece there by yourself … A big black man will walk up there and take your guitar, and he'll tune it. And then he'll play a piece and hand it back to you. That's the way I learned to play anything I want.

Those hundred words or so laid the groundwork for one of the most profound cases of mistaken identity in the history of American folklore. Tommy Johnson was not related to Robert Johnson, and although the two men are rumored by at least one source to have been acquainted and perhaps even played together on the odd occasion, there is little evidence that their lives intersected much more than this. No one on record claims to have heard either bluesman speak of the other. Tommy Johnson was older than Robert. Tommy was born in 1896 in Terry, Miss., and his 17 recordings were made nearly 10 years before those of Robert. In his day Tommy also was more popular than Robert, recording hits such as "Canned Heat Blues" and "Big Road Blues" for the Victor record label. Besides being blues musicians, the only other thing the two musicians seemed to have in common was a taste for strong liquor. Tommy Johnson, in fact, basically drank himself to death in 1956 after more than 40 years of chronic alcoholism.

The crossroads myth was intended for bluesman Tommy Johnson (1896-1956), who was no relation to Robert. Tommy Johnson's preacher brother, LeDell, told blues historian David Evans that he believed his brother sold his soul to the devil in exchange for musical talent.

Where did Tommy Johnson's brother LeDell come up with such a far-fetched story of Tommy selling his soul to the devil at the crossroads? LeDell Johnson was a former bluesman himself and converted to the ministry later in his life. It is a certainty that LeDell felt blues was the devil's music, as did virtually all of the Christian population in the state of Mississippi, although that never stopped some of the faithful from sipping a little sin once in awhile on a Saturday night.

In the same interview with David Evans, LeDell spoke of other brushes with apparitions from hell. However, Tommy Johnson had another brother, Mager, who totally rejected the notion that Tommy had sold his soul to the devil or anyone else. Perhaps it was Henry Townsend, a bluesman who knew Johnson well, who said it best: "That word 'devil' — you'd be surprised how effective it is." The word is so powerful, in fact, that it seemed to fit even better with the ascension of Robert Johnson, even though he never once mentioned to anyone that he was in league with the devil or that his dazzling musicianship had any root in a supernatural contract. Robert used the imagery of the devil in some of his most haunting and poetic music, but he also invoked the devil's name in fun as well. As writer Elijah Wald pointedly states in his book *Escaping the Delta*, the song "Me and the Devil Blues" is meant to be funny and provoke laughter, not fear and trembling.

There may have been a cultural disconnect with some of the early writers on Delta blues music who had not grown up immersed in a world of fire and brimstone as had most Mississippians. The lyrics of Robert Johnson's songs may have taken on an entirely different and more terrifying cast to those who were unfamiliar with tales of the devil and the ways in which Southern religion in particular adapts Biblical metaphors to suit the message. For example, a pastor at one church may paint the well-known story of Jesus' temptation by Satan in the wilderness in the most serious and sanctimonious of word pictures and another might milk the same story from a humorous point of view of Satan as a pest who won't go away. As an attorney might say, it's all in the context.

Johnson's juke-joint audiences would have been familiar with devil talk and its many shades of meaning. They probably didn't give a second thought to Johnson's depictive musings on the subject, certainly not enough to seriously believe he was actually in league with the devil. In one of his last interviews, Johnny Shines, when asked if he knew anything of Johnson's supposed pact with the devil at the crossroads answered, "He never told me that lie." Son House is alleged to have made an oblique reference to such a supernatural bargain in 1966, and that tiny snippet of a quote along with David Evans' interview with LeDell Johnson seem to be the underpinnings of the whole crossroads legend.

It was in an interview with Pete Welding in 1966 that Son House gave a crucial twist to the story we read earlier about how Johnson made an awful racket when first performing, yet six months later had improved almost miraculously. As Welding relates it: "House suggested in all seriousness that Johnson, in his months away from home, had 'sold his soul to the devil in exchange for learning to play like that.'"

That one reference, which Son House never repeated, is the only mention of Johnson and the devil by any of his contemporaries, including family members and former lovers. Biographers who have meticulously traced Johnson's timeline say that it was not six months, but at least two years before Johnson returned to the area where Son House was playing. A lot of beginning musicians get proficient on their instrument in that length of time. When the legend of the crossroads is stripped of its many rumors, innuendoes and might-have-beens, there isn't much left to hang a myth on.

The notion of selling one's soul to the devil in exchange for some deeply held desire is nothing new and in actuality goes back centuries in literature and legend. Perhaps best known is the tale of *Doctor Faustus* by Christopher Marlowe written in the late 1500s where a professor bargains away his soul to Mephistopheles in return for magical powers.

Niccolo Paganini (1782-1840) was a violinist of such astonishing virtuosity that people believed he could have only achieved such skill through supernatural means. He played with such ferocity and eccentric facial contortions that he seemed possessed by some unnatural force. Some observers claimed to see the devil standing next to him as he played. During his concerts members of the audience frequently fainted and wept as they watched him play — such was his effect on people. Paganini apparently rejected his demonic reputation, but the legend, like Johnson's, took hold. His life became almost a blueprint for other musicians similarly afflicted with extraordinary talent.

In the world of Delta blues, boasts about being on familiar terms with the devil were commonplace and sure to enhance one's reputation as being "bad." One performer in particular, Peetie Wheatstraw, capitalized on such rumors and advertised himself as the Devil's Son-In-Law, the High Sheriff from Hell. Flirtations with the devil in popular music range from Jelly Roll Morton to Mick

Jagger of the Rolling Stones to any number of present-day hip-hop and rock performers. Heavy metal icon Ozzy Osbourne, for instance, has practically made an industry of such dabblings. The popular country & western artist Charlie Daniels had a huge hit in 1979 with "The Devil Went Down To Georgia" about a fiddle player who goes head to head in a fiddling contest with the devil. What does the devil get if he wins? The fiddler's soul, of course. Despite all the bluster and posturing, few of these artists take all their devilment seriously. It's all show biz, and if we're honest we'll admit that it makes for some memorable songs.

Many writers have taken pains to trace the crossroads legend to West Africa and the widespread mythology there of Papa Legba, a keeper of the crossroads between this world and the otherworld. Anyone familiar with West African mysticism knows of the centuries-held beliefs in juju, their word for black magic. Even today a surprising number of West Africans — including the best-educated and most worldly — believe in the casting of spells, ghosts, witches, demonic possession and shape-shifting, where a human assumes the form of an animal.

Some of these beliefs became rooted in the New World among some African-Americans, particularly those from Haiti and other Caribbean enclaves where voodoo, a word derived in part from the African juju, was practiced. However, the beliefs became so intermingled with Christian mythology that they are often difficult to differentiate. Occasionally hoodoo (yet another derivation of the word juju) references surface in songs, such as Muddy Waters' classic "Got My Mojo Working," in which a man must go to Louisiana to buy a charm to put a spell on someone. Another is Screamin' Jay Hawkins' "I Put A Spell On You," in which the narrator explicitly tells a woman how he intends to keep her love. Notwithstanding these noteworthy exceptions, when most bluesmen sang about the devil and evil doings, they were speaking from a Christianized culture radically removed in many ways from West African lore.

In the song "Cross Road Blues," Johnson never discusses the crossroads as anything more magical than a backwoods way station where a hitchhiker might be more likely to "flag a ride" than by simply wandering down a lonesome highway. Johnson wasn't talking of hitching a ride with the devil. The drama and tension in the song come from the narrator's frustration at not finding a ride and the frightening possibility of being stranded in the dark: "Didn't nobody seem to know me/Everybody pass me by/Mmm, the sun goin' down, boy/dark gon' catch me here." A haunting song to be sure, but not one haunted by demons or devils.

Much — perhaps too much — has been read into the lyrics of Johnson's songs regarding the devil. As Henry Townsend said, that word "devil," it is mighty effective.

JOHN HAMMOND
RESURRECTS JOHNSON

A record selling only 5,000 copies in today's highly competitive music marketplace would be considered an outright flop. In the depths of the Great Depression, however, 5,000 copies in a regional market was a number large enough to get noticed. Some of the major record labels posted sales totals of only 100,000 units a year during those financially troubled times. Johnson's biggest record was "Terraplane Blues," a humorous double-entendre blues that slyly compared starting and driving a sleek Hudson Terraplane automobile with sexually stimulating a woman. It sold roughly 5,000 copies, mostly to rural African-Americans who favored blues. Undoubtedly the song, as well as the other 78s released by Johnson, found a larger audience on jukeboxes.

Even though Johnson's records were considered "race music" by the record companies and their distributors, the music found its way into the hands of a small, select group of whites who were avid collectors of jazz recordings. These jazz followers were typically educated, well read, middle or upper class and more liberal in their attitudes about race than the average white person. Magazines such as *downbeat*, still widely read today, covered the jazz world and its artists with an intellectual passion usually reserved for high-brow classical music. Many jazz fans followed blues as well, especially those blues vocalists who had swinging bands that were often comprised of some of the best jazz musicians.

John Hammond (Photo Copyright © 1994 Jim Marshall, courtesy of Stephen C. LaVere, Delta Haze Corporation Photographic Archive)

Those who delved even deeper into the so-called country blues, which usually featured an artist accompanying himself on guitar, were frequently surprised at the musical sophistication and poetic lyrics of these artists, who were often casually dismissed by others as "primitives."

Although Johnson himself could not have known, his recordings made their way into some influential hands. One was music critic Henry Johnson — which may or may not have been a pen name — who wrote for the publication *New Masses*. "We cannot help but call your attention to the greatest Negro blues singer who has cropped up in recent years … Johnson makes Leadbelly sound like an accomplished poseur." Another notice appeared in a British publication, *Melody Maker*, which stated: "Hot Springs' star is still Robert Johnson, who has turned out to be a worker on a [Robinsonville], Miss., plantation." Note that even before his death writers were getting the facts all wrong about Johnson.

Another jazz aficionado, one with a highly impressive pedigree, was John H. Hammond, a record producer for Columbia and other labels who was famous in music circles for discovering and championing such major jazz artists as Billie Holiday, Count Basie, Benny Goodman, Charlie Christian, Lionel Hampton, Lester Young and others. Several researchers believe Hammond actually wrote those first press notices about Johnson.

Hammond was an odd duck — an heir to the Vanderbilt fortune and a do-gooder who supported many left-wing political causes including an end to racial segregation, particularly in the world of music. Hammond was personally responsible for putting together mixed race jazz bands, encouraging, for example, the highly successful Benny Goodman to admit black pianist Teddy Wilson and black vibraphonist Lionel Hampton into his band. Hammond also was a founding investor in one of the first integrated nightclubs in America, Café Society in New York, where whites and blacks could sit together and enjoy mixed-race bands.

Long before Martin Luther King Jr. uttered his famous words "I have a dream," Hammond had his own vision of a world in harmony where blacks and whites, the East and West, North and South, and religions of all stripes could live together as one and appreciate rather than vilify their differences. His ideas weren't just empty rhetoric. He served more than 20 years on the board of directors of the National Association for the Advancement of Colored People (NAACP), a white man trusted and respected enough to retain this position through many political and social upheavals.

In his ideological war against those who would keep blacks in subservient roles, he fought hardest to introduce to the American public the great art of the American Negro. Because his talents lay primarily with music, it was music that allowed him to open the door to this better world he envisioned.

In 1938 Hammond came up with an idea to present the cream of African-American musicians, singers and composers to a diverse but sophisticated audience at Carnegie Hall, one of the greatest concert venues in the world. In his words he intended to "[show] the sources of black music and its evolution into today's jazz." It was a daunting task for anyone, even the indefatigable Hammond. Getting the talent was almost the least of his problems — he had contacts everywhere within the music industry. Getting someone to bankroll such a controversial undertaking — that was the big obstacle. Hammond received money from a family trust fund and had only limited access to the family's millions.

To no one's surprise Hammond was flat turned down by most would-be sponsors, including the NAACP. In 1938 the race issue was still too incendiary, even in the supposedly more enlightened culture of New York City. His eventual sponsor was a man named Eric Bernay, the publisher of a Marxist publication called *New Masses*. Although Hammond certainly considered himself a political liberal, he had long denounced communism as an unworkable, utopian ideal. He agreed to let *New Masses* underwrite the concert as long as they kept a low profile for their sponsorship and didn't use the concert for the purposes of political propaganda. Hammond and Bernay struck a deal and the show got underway.

Although jazz was foremost in Hammond's mind as the impetus for the concert, which was to be called "From Spirituals to Swing," he wanted to bring in all the African-American music genres and sub-genres that he felt influenced jazz and enriched its artistic worth. For example, he knew that the ecstatic voicings from black spirituals and gospel music had a direct impact on the often wild improvisatory flights of inspiration heard in the best jazz. He wanted his audience to explicitly understand these crucial connections and their history.

He felt that his evening should begin at the beginning — with some traditional West African chants from authentic field recordings from African villages. Hammond loved the trademark economical piano phrasings of Count Basie and penciled his band in. Next were three top-notch boogie-woogie pianists — Meade Lux Lewis, Albert Ammons and Pete Johnson with vocalist Big Joe Turner. He also brought in a proponent of stride piano with James

P. Johnson and Dixieland jazz with a band fronted by the legendary soprano saxophonist Sidney Bechet. There was gospel singing from the great Sister Rosetta Tharpe and spirituals by Mitchell's Christian Singers. Finally, he wanted some of the deeper Delta blues and chose Sonny Terry for a harmonica instrumental and a little known but highly evocative Mississippi singer/guitarist named Robert Johnson who was familiar to Hammond through the 78s released on Vocalion and associated labels.

Hammond felt that Johnson was the real thing — a tormented poet of the desolate Mississippi countryside who had fashioned a unique, mysterious vision and art from the bare living conditions in the often hostile environment of the Delta plantations. From the context of Hammond's later remarks, it is virtually certain that he saw Johnson as a raw, primitive folk genius with little or no professional experience outside his recordings. Hammond undoubtedly pictured Johnson as a sharecropper or farmhand who had fashioned his guitar style and plaintive singing from the sheer loneliness and frustration borne of being stuck in the middle of nowhere, oppressed by a white power structure and Jim Crow laws. It's fair to suggest that Hammond felt Johnson's great art rose out of necessity and a spiritual and cultural malaise. Hammond makes clear in his autobiography *John Hammond on Record* that the Deep South — the boondocks to New Yorkers and other urbanites — to him was not unlike countries of the Third World. He probably envisioned Johnson with calloused, work-hardened hands, wearing bib overalls and a straw hat and certainly not the suave, dapper, smoothly dressed dandy seen in the Hooks Brothers studio portrait of Johnson.

Hammond, who was nothing if not tenacious when it came to promoting the artists he felt were important, apparently dispatched one or more of his associates, perhaps Ernie Oertle of the ARC Recording Company, to locate Johnson and see to it that he was booked to perform at the "From Spirituals to Swing" concert.[9] The only fear Hammond had regarding Johnson was from record producer Don Law's inaccurate appraisal of Johnson as being too shy to perform and right "off the plantation." It isn't clear precisely who gave him the bad news, but Hammond received word that Johnson had just recently died, perhaps the result of murder. As he wrote in his book:

> Above all I wanted Robert Johnson as our male blues singer. Although he was virtually unknown to the general public, I considered him the best there was. We discovered, however, that earlier in the year he had been killed by his girl friend. Years later, when his records were reissued, he influenced artists as widely divergent as The Beatles, Bob Dylan, and the Rolling Stones. Ironically, his death occurred just as the blues he sang were becoming popular with jazz fans.

Clearly there was already confusion and myth-mongering regarding the death of Johnson. Like the Chinese whisper game, where one person whispers something to the person seated next to him who then whispers to the next person and so on, the last person to get the message often hears a wildly exaggerated version of the original whisper. It's not much of a stretch to see that the whisper game has played havoc with the facts of Johnson's life.

Big Bill Broonzy was the last-minute substitute for Johnson at the "From Spirituals to Swing" concert. However, Hammond took a moment to speak to his audience about Johnson's non-appearance:

> Robert Johnson was going to be the big surprise of the evening. I knew him only from his blues records and from the tall, exciting tales the recording engineers and supervisors used to bring about him from the improvised studios in Dallas and San

---

[9] According to researcher Steve LaVere, Hammond simply contacted Don Law.

Antonio. I don't believe that Johnson had ever worked as a professional musician anywhere, and it still knocks me over when I think of how lucky it is that a talent like his ever found his way to phonograph records ... Johnson died last week at the precise moment when Vocalion scouts finally reached him and told him that he was booked to appear at Carnegie Hall on December 23.

Hammond was an impresario who clearly wanted to impress. He, of course, knew full well that Johnson did not die at the "precise moment" the record scouts showed up at his door, but Hammond knew how to capitalize on the moment and make it memorable. To add further drama, Hammond, after making his short speech, produced a phonograph and played two of Johnson's songs, "Walking Blues" and "Preaching Blues," to his rapt audience. Since African-American music heard live was the whole reason behind "From Spirituals to Swing," it is all the more remarkable that John Hammond risked his audience's attention by playing records over the public address system.

Based on the press notices that followed, Hammond must have succeeded. Although Johnson was not specifically mentioned, *The New York Times* gave the concert a rave review, even pointing out the young MC's enthusiasm, "judging by his jitterbugging in his seat on stage." Not all of the artists on the bill that night at Carnegie Hall became household names afterward. Big Bill Broonzy remained a relatively minor figure in the world of blues as did Sonny Terry, who later had some small measure of success during the folk music boom of the sixties with partner Brownie McGhee. Although Johnson's music wasn't reissued for 20 more years, the concert still had a significant impact on a small but hugely influential coterie of writers and folklorists who would play a pivotal role in the resurrection of Johnson.

CHAPTER 8

A NEW AUDIENCE

B road, sweeping generalities about ethnic groups or minority populations seldom hold up under rigorous examination. To better understand how Robert Johnson went from being a marginal regional blues singer to a global phenomenon, however, we may need to sidestep this weakness of argument and plunge headlong into some of the perceived, if unprovable, differences in the ways blacks and whites regard music.

Veteran music writer Ed Ward once talked about scouring the many tiny record stands and shops in Kingston, Jamaica, for recent reggae singles and albums he had overlooked or had a hard time finding back in the States. He quickly discovered that if the records were much more than a month old, they weren't likely to be stocked any longer. "No mon, dat one finish. You wantin' de *old* songs," they would invariably tell him.

Almost as soon as sales of Johnson's last 78, which was released shortly after his death ("Love In Vain Blues" with "Preaching Blues" on the flip side), had declined, Johnson became yesterday's news to the Mississippi Delta blacks who had been his staple audience. Within a few years he was relegated to almost permanent obscurity in African-American culture, as had so many other bluesmen of the era, including Charley Patton, Tommy Johnson, Blind Lemon Jefferson and Leroy Carr. African-Americans, who found life arduous enough to live in the present, seldom were nostalgic for the past, including the music they had once celebrated and embraced. As a rule they were far more interested in what was new and original than something timeworn and old.

With many exceptions noted, African-Americans rarely actively supported music or musicians of a bygone era until the relatively recent rise of the black middle class. For example, the soul and rhythm and blues music of the 1950s and 1960s was forgotten practically overnight by African-Americans when disco and funk music became the rage in the 1970s. The Blues Brothers albums and movie — a largely white phenomenon — revived the careers of many neglected soul performers, from Sam and Dave to James Brown. Artists who had once played almost exclusively to black audiences found themselves selling out concerts to whites. By the new millennium, things had come almost full circle with more African-Americans exploring their roots music and cultural history than ever before. Today the music of James Brown, Ray Charles, Sam Cooke, Sly and the Family Stone and many others cuts across almost all social and racial demographics and is revered the world over.

Alan Lomax, seen here circa 1940s playing at a mountain music festival, was a folklorist who was instrumental in introducing the greater American public to blues and other folk musics. He also claimed to have met and interviewed Johnson's mother.

Yet in 1939, shortly after Johnson's death, it took the zeal and passion of a few obsessive whites to keep Johnson's music from passing into obscurity. In the history of American popular music, time after time it was the work of a handful of scholars and archivists foraging around in the cultural landfills of the past who managed to preserve our musical heritage. One such researcher was Alan Lomax, who helped introduce blues and Johnson to a much wider white audience. John Hammond got the ball rolling in 1938 when he played the music of Johnson to the audience at his historic "From Spirituals to Swing" Concert at Carnegie Hall. But it was Lomax who crisscrossed the American South with a 350-pound portable recording machine in the trunk of his car and did field recordings in the backwoods and shantytowns with the railroad gangs and prison inmates, where the music was actually being created. He didn't wait for the music to come to him.

Lomax, born in 1911, the same year as Johnson, was the son of one of America's first and most preeminent folklorists, John Lomax. It was John Lomax who discovered folk music icon Leadbelly at the Louisiana State Penitentiary in Angola, where he was serving time for murder. Both Lomaxes traveled the country making recordings for a historic undertaking by the Library of Congress. Alan Lomax, like his father, was interested in virtually all the ethnic music then flourishing (or dying out, as the case may be) in the United States, from Irish reels and jigs to German polkas. Although Alan Lomax captured the music of many social and ethnic groups in the country, he had a special place in his heart for the deep Delta blues of Mississippi.

John Hammond initially baptized him into the sound and spirit of Johnson. Hammond's enthusiasms were legendary — he enjoyed nothing more than converting others to his passionate interests in his favorite artists. Whereas Hammond was more interested in Johnson as a source, or one of the roots, of the jazz he favored, Lomax saw Delta blues in a different light. To Lomax, Johnson and some of the other Delta bluesman were "authentic" voices of the people. Part of the interest in American folk music stemmed from left-wing politics that held up the art of the oppressed masses — such as that of the American Negro — as being more relevant, honest, and "pure," than the deliberately elite aesthetics of the traditional European-based classical arts. Lomax, and those who followed in his footsteps, were interested in preserving history, not in making hit records. These preservationists have been accused of seeking museum relics like collectors of prized rare butterflies; however, if not for these archivists a lot of modern-day recordings would not exist. Older material is constantly being rediscovered and redeveloped by young, aspiring artists for new audiences.

Lomax was like a musical Johnny Appleseed — in a career that spanned five decades, he tirelessly explored little-known music forms and exposed them to the American public. Like so many others to come, Lomax wanted to know more about this enigma named Robert Johnson. With recording equipment in tow, he took off in his automobile to the cradle of the Delta blues in Mississippi in 1942. It took him 50-plus years to finally tell the story in his book *The Land Where the Blues Began*, but one of the first people he reports finding in his search for Johnson is Johnson's mother, whom he identifies as Mary Johnson. This story, like scores of others surrounding Johnson, is both weird and uncorroborated. We now know that Johnson's mother was Julia Majors Dodds (then named Julia Willis).

In the book, Lomax writes a long, impressionistic first-person account of meeting Johnson's mother. She tells him that she was at her son's side as he lay dying of poisoning and that his final request was for her to take his guitar from across his chest and hang it on the wall, because he finally realized that it was an instrument of the devil. Lomax last glimpsed Mary Johnson as she danced barefoot in her dusty yard "calling on the Lord and Little Robert."

It's one powerful story — one that asks the reader to swallow a lot of unverifiable information. At least three, possibly four, people claimed to have seen Johnson as he lay on his deathbed. Yet not one spoke of seeing the others there. And none of these people ever accurately identified where he was buried.

As important as Lomax was in cultivating and spreading the legacy of Delta blues, most biographers of Johnson are skeptical of the details of Lomax's story, particularly because Lomax didn't accurately cite the name of Julia Majors Dodds. Ultimately, the story may be just too far-fetched to be plausible.

The same year that Lomax blazed a trail through Tunica County in Mississippi in 1942, a group of music writers published a book called *The Jazz Record Book*. Geared towards fans of jazz, the writers wrote critiques of the available jazz records of the day, but still managed to include commentaries on some Delta blues recordings, including Johnson's "Terraplane Blues" and other songs. Although blighted by the usual number of inaccuracies, the authors nonetheless drew attention to Johnson's guitar playing ("as exciting as almost any in the folk blues field") and his "thrilling" singing.

Another jazz critic, Rudi Blesh, published a book in 1946 titled *Shining Trumpets: A History of Jazz*. Like *The Jazz Record Book*, Blesh focused primarily on jazz recordings but occasionally detoured into other musical arenas. He singled-out Johnson's "Hellhounds On My Trail" for discussion and his highly embroidered take on the song had a lingering, bone-chilling effect on folklorists to come. The impact of Blesh's dark, ghost-obsessed prose cannot be underestimated. It set the stage for the whole future industry of devils and bedevilment regarding Johnson. Here's what he wrote:

> The images — the wanderer's voice and its echoes, the mocking wind running through the guitar strings, and the implacable, slow, pursuing footsteps — are full of evil, surcharged with the terror of one alone among the moving, unseen shapes of the night. Wildly and terribly, the notes paint a dark wasteland, starless, ululant with bitter wind, swept by the chill rain. Over a hilltop trudges a lonely, ragged, bedeviled figure, bent to the wind, with his [guitar] held by one arm as it swings from its cord around his neck.

This narrative, more reminiscent of Stephen King or Edgar Allan Poe than the music reviews in *downbeat* or *Sing Out!* magazines, was guaranteed to attract attention. Blesh's Southern gothic description was cited dozens of times after the revival of Johnson's music in the 1960s and was a cornerstone of the emerging literature on the bluesman.

In the 1950s, nearly a decade after the publication of Rudi Blesh's ripple-effect descriptions, music in the United States underwent an overnight, seismic shift. This shift was called rock 'n' roll. Although rock 'n' roll was considered a youth music, its origins were complex. Folk music and blues both played a role, as did swing and jazz. But there was still no definitive book or reference source that tied all the sounds together. Nevertheless, this did not prevent the musical barriers from tumbling down.

CHAPTER 9

A GLOBAL PHENOMENON

I n the late 1950s, Elvis was in the army, Chuck Berry was in jail for transporting a prostitute across state lines, Jerry Lee Lewis was in exile for marrying his 13-year-old cousin, Little Richard had found religion and was studying to become a preacher, and Buddy Holly was killed in a plane crash. Rock 'n' roll itself seemed to have died, and although more and more whites were listening to black rhythm and blues, America was still in many ways culturally and musically segregated.

To college-bound youth, rock 'n' roll had become too much like "institutionalized adolescence," as one writer put it. It had become a sanitized, de-fanged product for teens that seldom held any promise of anything beyond puppy love and going steady. Many people were looking for a stronger dose of the real world in their music and weren't getting it from the pop charts, particularly if they were looking for anything with social relevance or something they could plumb for deeper intellectual meaning. Of course classical music, opera and jazz to some extent could answer some of those needs musically, but what if you were looking for songs that were a little more down to earth, something a hip student could feel was cool? What if you were sick and tired of music that was *wholesome*?

This was a time when American folk music broke out of the museums and union meeting halls and joined up with civil rights protesters, political leftists and students who wanted to escape what writer Gore Vidal once referred to as "a hell [that is] the American Way of Life." Of course, not all American college students were so dissatisfied or high-minded. They simply liked the more mature stories in the songs of folkies such as the Weavers and the Kingston Trio and the earnest, close vocal harmonies. There was also the grassroots appeal of vocalists standing on a stage with only a couple of acoustic guitars and getting an audience to clap and sing along. Such feel-good, sing-along concerts came to be known as "hootenannies."

Television came of age with Elvis and the early rock 'n' rollers, but the medium never seemed entirely comfortable with the music of this rebellious youth and limited it accordingly. Clean-cut white guys wearing button-down oxford shirts and khaki pants and strumming guitars that weren't plugged into loud amplifiers were much more palatable to the conservative social tastes of many American families than Chuck Berry duck walking across the stage or Jerry Lee Lewis literally setting his piano on fire. The politics and protests implicit in many of the folk songs ruffled relatively few feathers at the time because the sweet-voiced performers just seemed so darned nice compared to those greasy-haired, wild-eyed rock 'n' roll screamers who looked and acted more like truants than honor roll students.

Some folkies such as Bob Dylan devised their own brand of talking blues in which they would tell a long, rhyming story over a simple blues progression on acoustic guitar, punctuated with stabbing, venomous commentary on the problems in American society. Other folk singers such as Peter, Paul and Mary and Simon and Garfunkel wedded pop song melodies and sensibilities to the folk tradition and created a commercial product acceptable to youth as well as older generations.

The mainstream acceptance of folk music caused a lot of the hardcore folk purists to dig deeper into America's many folk musics searching for more "authenticity." It was at this time that hundreds if not thousands of American college students began rediscovering some of the still-living original Delta bluesmen,

especially those whose music
seemed a good fit in the
world of acoustic folk music:
Sleepy John Estes, Mississippi
John Hurt and Mance
Lipscomb. Leadbelly and Josh
White already had become
popular among white college
students and played often at
the coffeehouses where
students, many of whom
were too young to drink
alcohol legally, gathered to
hear folk music. "Folk blues"
or "country blues" began to
have a recognizable following
and record companies began
catering more and more to
those tastes. Bluesmen such as

Leadbelly (real name Huddie
Ledbetter) was a pivotal figure in the
folk blues revival of the 1950s and
1960s. Folk music fans who liked his
acoustic blues often discovered deep
Delta blues artists such as Robert
Johnson.

Sonny Terry and Brownie McGhee, Lightnin' Hopkins, Bukka
White, Son House and Skip James were dusted off and brought
back into the firmament.

A book titled simply *Country Blues* by writer/musician Samuel
Charters came out in 1959 that finally tied together the histories of
pre-War blues, post-War blues, early jazz, rhythm and blues, Negro
spirituals, gospel and folk music. Even more important, a record
album was released in conjunction with the book that included cuts
from several long-lost bluesmen. A track by Robert Johnson,
"Preaching Blues," was included, the first reissue of any of his
songs in 20 years. Charters' far-reaching book and the
accompanying record set the stage for the blues revival of the 1960s
and brought a laser-like focus to the life and artistry of Johnson.

In 1961 Columbia Records, which owned the masters and
available metal parts of all the Johnson recordings, decided to
release one LP of 16 selected tracks to be called *Robert Johnson: King*

of the Delta Blues Singers.[10] John Hammond was instrumental in creating this album. A folk blues revival in the United States was already underway and what better time than 1961 to reintroduce to the American public the long-forgotten songs of one of the greatest and most phantom-like country blues singers of all time. Frank Driggs was chosen to produce the LP and write the liner notes, and the information he subsequently provided was the match that lit the fuse of the Johnson explosion soon to come. For all practical purposes, Driggs' notes were the first writings all but an insular handful of Americans had ever seen on the subject of Johnson. To those finding *King of the Delta Blues Singers* in the bins of record stores, Johnson was something new, a buried treasure, a revelation, not something old and familiar.

Since no one at the time had ever seen a photograph of Johnson, an artist, the renowned Burt Goldblatt, was commissioned to illustrate the cover of *King of the Delta Blues Singers*. The cover art itself has become an iconic tableau in the legacy of Johnson, an evocative, expressionistic take of an almost faceless black man sitting in a chair hunkered down over an acoustic guitar. As if the viewer is observing Johnson from the heavens, the perspective is looking down upon the figure in the illustration in what professional illustrators sometimes refer to as a "down shot." Although *King of the Delta Blues Singers* was only modestly successful as a reissue, selling around 10,000 to 15,000 copies over the next 10 years according to one source, its influence on musicians and future writers was powerful. Bob Dylan, who was signed to Columbia Records in 1961, said this after hearing Johnson for the first time:

> From the first note the vibrations from the loudspeaker made my hair stand up. The stabbing sounds from the guitar could almost

---

[10]According to recording engineer Steve Lasker, who has worked extensively with the remastering of the Johnson catalog, a number of long-missing metal parts were finally located at Sony Music — hidden in the back of a closet.

break a window. When Robert Johnson started singing, he seemed like a guy who could have sprung from the head of Zeus in full armor. I immediately differentiated between him and anyone else I had ever heard. The songs weren't customary blues songs. They were perfected pieces — each song contained four or five verses, every couplet intertwined with the next but in no obvious way … They jumped all over the place in range and subject matter, short punchy verses that resulted in some panoramic story — fires of mankind blasting off the surface of this spinning piece of plastic … .

A year later Dylan became one of the first whites to publicly perform a song of Johnson's, in this case "Rambling On My Mind" at the Finjan Club in Montreal, Canada.

Bob Dylan wasn't the only young white folk musician to develop an obsession with Johnson. John Paul Hammond, the son of producer John Hammond, the man who first introduced Johnson to the world at his "From Spirituals to Swing" concert in 1938, had developed a devotion to country blues as a teenager. As the senior Hammond told the story in his autobiography: "I was preparing to reissue an album by Robert Johnson, the great blues singer who had died in the

Bob Dylan may have been the first marquee-name white artist to play a Johnson song for a crossover audience in 1962 in Montreal.

late 1930s, before he had become widely known (and before I could get him for "From Spirituals to Swing"). I sent [my son] an acetate of the Johnson album and he was tremendously impressed. He had his musical hero at last and knew how he wanted to sing himself."

John Paul Hammond was probably the first white to record a song of Johnson's. The song was "Crossroads Blues" (sic) and was featured on Hammond's debut album in 1963, a song that was later to be recorded more famously by Eric Clapton in the group Cream. He included at least one Johnson cover on almost every subsequent album he released in that decade. More than 40 years later, John Paul Hammond is still recording Johnson tunes and playing them to appreciative audiences around the world.

John Paul Hammond (Courtesy of Vanguard Records, a Welk Music Group Company)

Yet what about those people who lived on the other side of the tracks, in Chicago's South Side, Harlem in New York, East St. Louis, South Los Angeles, Detroit, Beale Street, the piney woods and Delta flatlands of Mississippi? What of the African-Americans who brought this music to life in the first place? To answer these questions and understand how the blues of African-Americans evolved separately from the newfound interest of white patrons, we need to go back in time again.

Mechanical cotton pickers were introduced into the Mississippi Delta as early as the 1930s. They were extraordinarily expensive, troublesome, and didn't pick cotton as cleanly or rapidly as the sharecroppers who for generations had provided the hand labor for this difficult-to-harvest crop. During World War II, however, the need for factory workers was so great that waves of black sharecroppers left the cotton fields for the greener, colder pastures up North. Those sharecroppers comprised a Great Migration out of Mississippi and other parts of the South. They resettled north in Memphis, St. Louis, and especially in Detroit and Chicago to work in the factories, mills and munitions plants that were in 24-hour operation to meet the industrial needs of the war effort.

Although African-American soldiers fought and died heroically in World War II, racial barriers kept many out of the armed forces and few were allowed to fight side by side with whites. Economically, however, this was a historic break with the past for thousands of African-Americans. Many found good-paying, steady jobs for the first time in their lives and were able to feed and clothe their families and live in housing several steps above the tar-paper shacks that were the burden of life as sharecroppers.

Soon after World War II, the mechanical cotton picker was perfected and came down in price. As early as 1935, one of the key inventors of the mechanical picker, John Rust, had predicted that "the sharecropper system of the Old South will have to be abandoned." Barely 10 years after making this statement every mechanical cotton picker sold displaced from 50 to 100 sharecroppers, not to mention their families. These people left en masse for the promised land of the American industrial North.

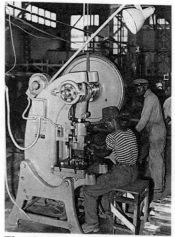

The desperate need for factory workers during World War II prodded scores of African-Americans to leave the Delta cotton fields for the promised land of America's industrial North.

Field hands and their families, who had often grown up in abject, subsistence level poverty with no electricity or running water, found themselves in seething metropolises such as Chicago, crowded into tenement buildings, yet finding life better than it was back in the South.

These African-Americans brought their music tastes with them and adapted them to big city ways. The nightclubs of the big city were unimaginably bigger and louder than the tiny juke joints out in the middle of the Mississippi nightfall. To be heard over the racket, the bluesmen who had previously played simple acoustic instruments — instruments that they could carry on their backs — began using electric guitars and amplifiers. Because a singer couldn't be heard too well by himself, he often had a band to back up the beat to get the people out of the shadows of the nightclub booths and onto the dance floor.

The sound was new, yet the music was familiar, and the volume was overpowering. While whites listened to folk blues artists in quiet coffeehouses (some white hipsters would actually applaud by snapping their fingers), artists like Muddy Waters and Howlin' Wolf, who had begun playing blues in Mississippi when Johnson was still alive, were blowing the doors off the hinges in the lounges and clubs of the South Side in Chicago where white folks seldom ventured.

Every mechanical cotton picker, such as the one shown here on the Hopson Plantation in Clarksdale, Mississippi in 1944, displaced from fifty to one hundred sharecroppers. (Photograph courtesy of *The* (Memphis) *Commercial Appeal*)

Two of Johnson's songs in particular were retooled and amped-up by the new wave of electrified urban bluesmen — "Sweet Home Chicago" and "Dust My Broom." "Sweet Home Chicago" became a staple of rhythm and blues performers throughout the United States, as it remains to this day. "Dust My Broom" was reinvigorated by a Delta bluesman who famously electrified slide guitar until it became his screaming, slashing musical signature — Elmore James. James was born in 1918 in Richland, Miss., and played on the same street corners and in the same roadhouse joints as Johnson, Son House and Johnny Shines. But he was little noticed until later in life, when he plugged his guitar into an amplifier and cut loose on the new, improved "Dust My Broom" for the Trumpet record label. James used the "Dust My Broom" slide riff on dozens of other songs and his recordings became jukebox and radio station fixtures to untold numbers of black Americans. Few, however, identified "Sweet Home Chicago" and "Dust My Broom" as songs by Johnson, now long dead and long forgotten.

The electric guitar became a lead instrument rather than just an instrument for rhythmic accompaniment. Such players as T-Bone Walker, Gatemouth Brown and a young Memphian named B.B. King began to incorporate jazz stylings into their playing and using single notes rather than chords to accent and echo their vocal effects. By turning up the volume on the amplifiers, these guitarists discovered that it not only made their music louder but changed the ringing, chiming tone of an electric guitar to something far more biting, stinging and attention-getting. This became the new sound of the electric guitar, and young white guitar players likewise began to see the almost limitless possibilities of the instrument.

As more and more white college students began to drift away from the softer, politer sounds of folk music

In the 1950s the electric guitar (being played here by Calvin Newborn) became a lead instrument rather than a background instrument for rhythmic accompaniment. (Photo courtesy of Memphis Finest/The First Family of Memphis's Jazz)

toward something more immediate and aggressive, many discovered that a simple switch of the radio dial would put them into a new world of blues, fashioned with a beat and drive and modern sound far removed from the gentle folk blues of the coffeehouse circuit. Radio stations with programming for black, urban audiences began to notice a lot of white listeners tuning in and phoning in requests for rhythm and blues numbers. A few intrepid blues fanatics began to take field trips to the Mississippi Delta, going door to door searching for obscure blues 78s.

Some of the more curious, such as Paul Butterfield and Mike Bloomfield in Chicago, were brave enough to run the gauntlet of hard stares as they walked the streets of the South Side looking for blues joints that would allow them in. These young white blues fans began forming their own bands and playing the music themselves, and it was only a short time before they were asking to sit in on late night jam sessions at the clubs and lounges where the new electrified blues flourished, shocking many of the local customers who never expected to see whites playing *their* music on *their* turf.

These students of blues were thrilled to sit at the feet of the veteran blues masters, the men they had worshipped from afar. Then, as now, there was criticism of whites playing blues — cries that it was the black man's music and could only be properly understood and played by blacks. This line of thinking presupposed that blues descended directly from West African music that was then filtered exclusively through the African-American experience. As discussed in the Preface, however, this was not always the case. There was always a great deal of musical cross-pollination in American music, and Johnson played the so-called hillbilly blues of Jimmie Rodgers as well as popular songs by crooners such as Bing Crosby. Jukeboxes in the Mississippi juke joints stocked a wealth of music, far more than just blues. Moreover, to think of blues as a pure and "untainted" ethnic music is simply wrong historically. Whites always sang blues and worked side by side with blacks in the fields of the Delta, and blacks likewise assimilated many other music forms into blues, just as Hawaiian steel guitar playing influenced blues slide guitar.

Music writers generally agree that many of the young white blues players introduced a harder rock-'n'-roll flavored edge to their version of blues. Some of these bands, such as The Paul Butterfield Blues Band, were integrated — Butterfield was a white singer and harp player and his band consisted of two white guitarists, a white keyboard player, a black drummer and a black bassist. They created a sensation in the blossoming world of white blues and eventually gained respect among their African-American blues idols as well.

On the other side of the Atlantic, in Great Britain in particular, musical shock waves also were being felt. American seamen who docked along the shores of the United Kingdom often brought their American records with them and sometimes sold them at record markets in cities such as London and Liverpool. There had been a folk boom in England that paralleled the one in the U.S. and just as in America the fans of this music eventually wanted to dig deeper in hopes of finding something grittier and more meaningful. To many young Brits, American blues music was the most soulful, stirring, pulse-pounding music they had ever heard. Nothing else had ever sounded so cool. Writer Peter Guralnick put it this way:

> The thing that should never be underestimated is the allure of the "cool." The point is, the very fact that it wasn't known and the fact that it had bubbled up from underneath and the fact that it grew out in these sort of ripples ... Everybody says it had to come over from England. Well, I don't think that's true. It came from many different directions. [It was] certainly kept alive in this country as it was in England. But it definitely came over also through the Rolling Stones and through Eric Clapton. Everybody knew this was cool. This was the *ultimate* cool.

The ultimate cool. That is exactly what Eric Clapton must have thought as he first listened to Johnson. We have already discussed how Clapton energized several of Johnson's songs while a member of John Mayall's Bluesbreakers and Cream and how the Rolling Stones popularized "Love In Vain" on two of their LPs.

You might say that the atom was split at that point. After Clapton and the Stones introduced Johnson to a mass market around the world, others soon followed: Led Zeppelin, Canned Heat, Steve Miller, Fleetwood Mac. As of this writing, there are hundreds of bands that have covered Johnson songs, and in virtually every corner of the world Johnson is being played live in some blues club or being broadcast on the radio. There are probably more downloads of Johnson songs from the Internet every day than he ever sold in his lifetime. Eric Clapton recently recorded an entire album of Johnson tunes titled *Me and Mr. Johnson*, in

Modern day juke joint. (Photo courtesy of Bill Steber)

tribute to the man who most inspired him. Johnson has earned a permanent place in American music.

Today, blues still has many definitions. To some it is high-volume, hard-rocking white virtuosos with tricked out guitars like the late Stevie Ray Vaughn. To others it is an old black man perched on a stool playing acoustic folk blues. Or jazz-flavored and played with brass instruments. Or raunchy grind music played in sweaty rhythm-and-blues bars. Or a front-porch musician like R. L. Burnside in the North Mississippi hill country who still knows how to cut a man, cuss his woman and drink hard liquor all night long.

THE MOVIE THAT CHANGED THE LEGEND

Although blues scholars have been slow to acknowledge it, the 1986 movie *Crossroads* starring Ralph Macchio, who is best known for his lead role in the *Karate Kid* film series, may have done more to introduce the world to the legend of Robert Johnson than the cover versions of Johnson's songs recorded by Eric Clapton and the Rolling Stones. *Crossroads*, directed by Walter Hill, was by no means a blockbuster movie at the box office and it won few industry awards or kudos from critics, but its near-continuous rotation on cable television in the years after its initial release put it in the living rooms and minds of millions of viewers worldwide.

The film begins with a stark black and white sequence showing an actor portraying Johnson standing at the proverbial crossroads in Mississippi. Johnson, wearing a suit and string tie and carrying a guitar walks down a gravel path seemingly in the middle of nowhere, the landscape a bleak, flat nothingness. When he comes to the crossroads, where another gravel path intersects with the one he is walking down, he stops and looks around nervously, as the wind howls and the film fades to black.

Readers will recall that this scenario is the very one that LeDell Johnson related about his brother Tommy Johnson. In the film's next sequence — shot in color rather than black and white — we see the young Johnson walking down the hallway of an aging hotel. He knocks tentatively at a door and a white man lets him in, a recording engineer. The engineer asks him if he has ever recorded before and Robert shakes his head no. The engineer then tells him he only needs to sit in front of the microphone and play his heart out.

True to the legend, Robert sits in a chair with his back to the engineer. The engineer then goes into an adjoining room where he starts the recording process. Robert takes a quick drink of whiskey, puts a metal slide on his finger and begins to play some dazzling slide guitar followed by the words to "Cross Road Blues." The inference, if one catches it, is that Robert's obvious mastery of his guitar came about as the result of something sinister and supernatural that happened back at the crossroads.

The scene then shifts to the present where Ralph Macchio, who is later dubbed Lightning Boy, picks up a cassette tape of *Robert Johnson: King of the Delta Blues Singers* and loads it into his player. The crux of the story that follows is that Lightning Boy, a Juilliard-trained whiz kid on classical guitar, has a closet passion for Johnson and blues. He has researched the life of Johnson and believes that there is a missing song that Johnson never recorded. He aims to get the song by tracking down Johnson's friend and fellow musician, a fictionalized Willie Brown, who he believes will know the song.

Lightning Boy finds Willie Brown at a nursing home in New York (the real life Willie Brown died in 1952). Willie Brown is a haunted, embittered old man whose soul, like Johnson's, has been signed away to the devil, a tall, grinning black man called Scratch. After a series of misadventures on the road, Lightning Boy and Willie Brown arrive at a Mississippi juke joint where Lightning Boy is to "cut heads" or compete with another guitar player who is in league with Scratch. The climactic scene pits the two guitarists against each other on stage with the souls of both Willie Brown and Lightning Boy at stake.

With Scratch grinning in the audience, the competing guitar player, a long-haired white rocker (Steve Vai) with a screaming, full-shred style, at first seems like he is going to wipe the floor with the shy and nervous Lightning Boy. In a move that many blues fans who watched the movie found irritating, if not offensive, Lightning Boy abandons his blues playing at the crucial moment and whips out some of his Juilliard-trained classical licks, which the competitor cannot duplicate. The rocker quits in disgust and throws his guitar to the floor, a sign of defeat. And so two souls are rescued from the jaws of the hellhounds and Scratch is no longer smiling.

Crossroads has had an enduring popularity and the notion of selling one's soul at an isolated crossroad in return for musical greatness has, to borrow from writer Kenneth Tynan, "[sunk] a pipeline to the depths of the American unconscious." It wouldn't be too far-fetched to say that a majority of today's students, by the time they reach high school, are familiar with at least some part of the Johnson myth, even if they do not immediately connect with the name or readily identify his music.

In the mid-1980s the public had not yet seen a photograph of Johnson or listened to anything more than the 29 songs that had been released only on vinyl and cassette tape. As 1990 approached, all that was to change.

THE FEUD OVER THE JOHNSON PHOTOS

The story of Robert Johnson is filled with intrigue and subplots, and one of the most fascinating is an odd contest of wills between blues researcher Mack McCormick and music historian Stephen LaVere. McCormick, a resident of Houston, Texas, for many years, reportedly was on the trail of Johnson as early as 1948. As one of the earliest authorities on blues, he began to produce records for rediscovered bluesmen, including Lightnin' Hopkins, and write the occasional article or essay for publications such as *downbeat*. Eventually he performed field work in various capacities for the Smithsonian Institution. His real purpose in life, so it would seem, was to obsessively track down every possible lead he could to unearth information about Johnson.

In 1972 McCormick stumbled upon Johnson's half-sister Carrie Thompson, who was living in Churchton, Md., a suburb of Washington, D.C. There is little argument that McCormick was first on the scene. What he found at Carrie Thompson's house was the Holy Grail of blues—a photograph of the most mysterious figure in the history of American popular music, Robert Johnson. Believing there was only one photograph, he struck an agreement of sorts with Carrie Thompson and left with enough new raw material on Johnson's life to write the definitive biography — one he intended to call *Biography of a Phantom*. But McCormick never wrote the book. He also failed to make use of the borrowed Johnson photograph.

In 1973, one year later, music historian Stephen LaVere talked with Carrie Thompson on the phone. When asked if she had any photographs of Johnson, she replied, "It's funny you should ask. I had lost it for a long time, but I found it in a Bible." Soon thereafter LaVere drove from Memphis to Washington D.C. to meet with Thompson.

Like McCormick, LaVere was a devout collector of blues 78s and had produced blues and other recordings for Liberty Records, including some of the highly acclaimed Legendary Masters series. In 1969 he hired on with the Memphis Country Blues Festival, which held an annual blues event for several years. During this time he met some of the living legends of blues: Bukka White, Furry Lewis, Sleepy John Estes and many others. Like Mack McCormick before him, Steve LaVere eventually embarked on a lifelong personal crusade, not to find the meaning of life or some other far-flung philosophical notion, but to find the meaning of Robert Johnson. And perhaps to make a little money as well.

Author Peter Guralnick is one of the few writers to penetrate Mack McCormick's wall of silence. In his book *Searching for Robert Johnson,* Guralnick whets the appetite in his detailed and lyrical description of the photographs McCormick showed him. One of the photos is of Julia Majors Dodds, Robert's mother, and another is of his half-brother Charles Leroy. A third is of Johnson standing next to a relative, a nephew, in a sailor's uniform. This is the fabled "third photo," which apparently hasn't been seen by any outside eyes since McCormick revealed it to Guralnick.

When Steve LaVere visited Carrie Thompson in 1973, she showed him the Hooks Brothers portrait and other family photos, but no shot of Johnson standing next to a nephew in a sailor's uniform. While rummaging through an old cedar chest with Thompson, LaVere discovered a tiny photo that turned out to be the photo booth self-portrait of a somber-looking Johnson holding his guitar and staring coldly into the lens with a cigarette angling sharply downward from his lips (see cover of this book). The photo was as small as a postage stamp, slightly blurred, and not nearly as artistically posed as the Hooks Brothers portrait, but its moodiness certainly seemed to echo the hellhound-haunted artist many people envisioned in Johnson.

LaVere, who wasn't shy and was indisputably more savvy regarding the legalities of copyright ownership than his rival Mack McCormick, struck up a bargain with Carrie Thompson: He would form a company to copyright the photographs as well as the Johnson songs and for 50 percent of royalties and other monies would oversee all the Johnson holdings. LaVere knew that history was waiting for any visual proof of Johnson's existence and would pay dearly for such proof. He also suspected that the Johnson songbook could possibly be worth millions in both future royalties and the back royalties that could be demanded from the many artists who had recorded Johnson's songs essentially for free while they were listed as material in the public domain.

LaVere contacted Columbia Records to let them know of the existence of the Johnson photographs and to let them know that he and the Johnson family were claiming ownership rights to the songs and photos. In his article "The Plundering of Robert Johnson," writer Robert Gordon states that John Hammond, the legendary producer who initially exposed Johnson to the American public in his "From Spirituals to Swing" concert, chose not to contest LaVere's assertions and instead willingly obliged his requests. Hammond was likely just as excited about the prospect of Johnson photographs as the bluesman's legion of admirers. LaVere and Hammond discussed reissuing the Johnson albums with the recently discovered photographs on their covers, but instead decided to produce a box set of all the recordings. As the project neared completion in the summer of 1975, McCormick ended his silence.

After discovering that he had been trumped by LaVere, he did what many Americans do when faced with such a dicey dilemma — he threatened to sue. Adding insult to injury, John Hammond at this time claimed he didn't remember McCormick and had no recollection of ever speaking to him about Johnson photographs. It should be noted here that Hammond had suffered a heart attack and his memory may have been affected. Johnson's recordings weren't considered enough of a bullet-proof property in the 1970s to warrant such thorny legal entanglements. So Columbia Records declined to reissue Johnson, photos or not. For more than 15 years Johnson lay idle, a subject to be brought up periodically at the staff meetings at Columbia Records only to be quickly shot down as too much legal trouble. McCormick surprised everyone by abandoning all claims to Johnson. No one really knows why. No one knows if he still has that third photo of Johnson or if he really knows the man who allegedly murdered Johnson.

In 1986, events turned in LaVere's favor again when he allowed *Rolling Stone* magazine to publish a copy of the photo booth self-portrait of Johnson after the Rock and Roll Hall of Fame and Museum in Cleveland included Johnson in its first ever group of inductees (under the category "early influences"). The small image of Johnson buried on page 48 of the February 13, 1986, issue of *Rolling Stone* finally allowed millions of people around the world to see with their own eyes what Johnson really looked like.

McCormick didn't sue.

Stephen LaVere pressed forward with his resurrection of Johnson. The Hooks Brothers photograph of Johnson turned up twice in 1989, in an obscure publication called *78 Quarterly* devoted to collectors of old 78 rpm records and more significantly on the front cover of Peter Guralnick's short biography, *Searching for Robert Johnson*.

Compact discs were not available in the United States prior to 1983. The first recordings released in this medium, which no one could predict in terms of popularity and profitability, were of classical music and high-end audio jazz meant to show off the dynamics of the supposed better sound quality. The first discs cost more than $20 each ($40 in today's money), which was four times the price of a typical vinyl LP. Record companies had seen new technology come and go — reel-to-reel tapes and eight-tracks to

name but two — and they weren't at first ready to sink millions
into CD reissues of their product lines.

Making matters even worse, the first compact disc players were
greatly overpriced and compact discs of popular music often
sounded far worse than their LP counterparts. CDs were supposed
to have sound quality superior to that of LPs, but audio enthusiasts
were reporting just the opposite. It took several years for the record
companies to get the hang of CD remastering. Finally, they were
releasing CDs that rivaled LPs in regard to audio fidelity, and they
began to expand their product lines. The public's taste gradually
began to shift toward CDs and something unexpected happened:
albums that had been out of print for years were in demand again
because customers wanted their favorite old recordings in the new
compact disc format.

Reissues of old rock 'n' roll standbys such as Bill Haley and the
Comets, Buddy Holly and Chuck Berry sold thousands more copies
than record companies ever imagined — sales of those artists'
music had been dormant for years, but CDs brought them back
from life support. When the Beatles' old albums were finally
reissued on CD after a wait of several long years the news was
broadcast worldwide.

Record companies were turning their vaults inside out to make
money on product they thought had flat-lined. At the end of the
1980s, only a few major artists hadn't been reissued on compact
disc, and Robert Johnson was at the top of the list. In 1990
CBS/Columbia Records released a double CD box set: *Robert
Johnson: The Complete Recordings*. In the promotional materials sent
to the media, the two known photographs of Johnson were
included with specific instructions on permission for use. The
photos had to be identified with proper copyright symbols and
dates and notification that the photos were copyrighted by Stephen
C. LaVere. The photos also could only be used without charge if
they were to accompany an article or review specifically about *The
Complete Recordings*. If a magazine used either photograph to
accompany a biographical article about Johnson or about Delta

blues in general or any other subject not specifically about the CD box set, the editors were informed that they were in violation of the agreement and were asked to pay royalties. Even more controversial was LaVere's decision to press for royalties when an artist did a likeness or rendering of Johnson based on the copyrighted photographs. Several magazines, including *Musician*, were asked to pay royalties for including illustrations of Johnson on their covers.

To no one's surprise, LaVere was practically stoned in print by the tight-knit world of blues historians for attempting to make money off such sacred relics as the only known photographic images of Johnson. Many reacted as if he had committed heresy against a figure of high holiness. But others point out that under LaVere's control, the legacy of Johnson has been preserved and, indeed, has flourished.

McCormick never published his *Biography of a Phantom*. He was last seen in the 1992 documentary, *The Search for Robert Johnson*, where, among other things, he discusses the devil myth as it relates to Johnson. In an article in *Texas Monthly* in 2003, McCormick would say only one thing about Johnson — that he no longer had any interest in the bluesman.

The self-portrait that is on the cover of this book was the first Johnson photograph ever seen by the public and, as mentioned earlier, was published in 1986 in an issue of *Rolling Stone* magazine. Johnson looks moody and one can practically hear the wind cry and feel the hellhounds close at heel. It seems to conjure every image blues writers ever had of the tortured demon-haunted Delta genius that many hold so dear. It is a photograph that deepens the mystery.

He is not dressed up here, and one cannot help but wonder why he took a photograph of himself, even if it was only in a photo booth, in his shirtsleeves with his shirt open at the neck and suspenders clearly visible. Johnson was known to one and all as a smart dresser, a man, as Johnny Shines said, who could hobo on a long train ride and still look freshly pressed when he got off.

The lazy eye that several people mentioned who knew Johnson is very apparent here. Some writers have surmised that he may have had a cataract in his left eye, causing it to swell and close slightly. Others have said that Johnson did not go farther in his schooling because of bad eyesight, the result of a bad eye from early childhood or birth. It has also been suggested that Johnson wore eyeglasses on occasion, but if he did it was only in private and never around fellow musicians, fellow travelers or his audiences. He also apparently did not have glasses with him when he recorded in Texas.

In this photo, Johnson is cradling his guitar, in this case a Kalamazoo KG-14, and chording it with his fret hand, his long, "spider-like" fingers positioned almost identically to his Hooks Bros. shot. What isn't typically mentioned is that Johnson has a capo fixed on the second fret of his guitar. A capo is a sort of clamp that presses down on the strings across a fret allowing a guitarist to vary the key he wishes to play in. This without question factored significantly into Johnson's playing technique and his sound.

It appears as if a plain white sheet is used as the backdrop for the photograph, underscoring the humble setting. The photo was reportedly taken in 1933, a couple of years prior to the Hooks Bros. portrait, which would mean Johnson was in his early 20s. His hair is cut short, the hairline receding somewhat from his forehead. He is slight, small, and even though he was a lover not a fighter, you can't tell it by the stony look on his face, which could be a model for the hostile scowls seen on many hip-hop CDs.

Henry and Robert Hooks, who were from a prominent African-American family in Memphis, established a photography studio in 1907 and eventually moved to an office on Beale Street where they became the photographers of choice for blacks throughout the Mid-South.

One such client was Johnson, who scheduled an appointment sometime in 1935, a year prior to his recording contract with ARC. From the way Johnson is dressed and posed, it is obvious he took this photo session with the utmost seriousness.[11] Johnson looks directly into the camera eye with supreme confidence; there is no shyness in his demeanor. This is undoubtedly his "show" face, the one he presented his audiences, with a winning, tooth-filled grin and a direct "here-I-am" twinkle in his eye that must have won him the acquaintance of a number of female admirers.

In this photo, perhaps more than the dime-store shot, we can appreciate the reports of his handsomeness and the persona of a blues dandy he purposely projects. How do we know he was identifying himself as a bluesman? How many musicians bring their instruments with them for formal studio portraits? Few, unless the purpose of the picture is for publicity, which was not the case here. In the two photos of Johnson that have surfaced, he is holding his guitar in both. This is not insignificant. It tells us not only who he was, but who *he thought* he was. Even in 1935 at the famed Hooks Bros. studio, Johnson was inseparable from his music. There he is, bigger than life, playing (in this case) a late 1920s Gibson L-1 guitar. The guitar looks weathered and road-weary and stands in stark contrast to the sharp-dressed man holding it.[12]

Everything else seems brand spanking new, from the fedora hat cocked just so down to his spit-shined black dress shoes. Although Johnson probably never had more than a hundred dollars in his pocket at any one time, the pin-striped suit he is wearing belies this and looks tailored and expensive and fits him expertly. His well-creased pants bespeak a man who paid strict attention to his appearance and was meticulous about his style. The necktie is knotted and flared well enough to do the Duke of Windsor proud. A white handkerchief doesn't merely peek out of his jacket pocket,

---

[11]The Hooks Bros. Studio Portrait can be viewed at www.deltahaze.com.

[12]Steve LaVere points out that there is no way of knowing for sure if the guitars in the photographs actually belonged to Johnson.

it extends way out into a knife's point, a stamp of his own personal taste.

Johnson's long, graceful fingers are seen actively playing his guitar—one hand in a chord position, the other thumbing and finger-picking the strings. Although he used a metal or glass tube of some kind when he played slide guitar, he chose not to have it on his fret hand for this photograph.

For those who saw the dime-store photograph first, the Hooks Bros. portrait came as a bit of a shock. The smile, the confidence, the natty clothes—none of these things propped up the image of Johnson as a tormented folk poet filled with anguish, sorrow and lament. This image was much closer in mind to the man having fun singing "They're Red Hot" than "Hellhounds On My Trail." This photo alone caused a lot of people to readjust their thinking about Johnson. It stripped away the veneer of mystery so many fancied about the legend of Johnson.

A third photo is said to exist, but only members of Johnson's family, blues researcher Mack McCormick, writer Alan Greenberg, and author Peter Guralnick have seen it. Guralnick's description of the photograph appears in his book *Searching for Robert Johnson* and is reprinted with the author's permission below:

> The next photograph shows a young man in a sailor's uniform, obviously pleased, obviously proud, with another man, very slightly older, standing beside him, his arm draped affectionately around the sailor's shoulder. The sailor, Mack McCormick tells me, is Robert's nephew, Louis, at home in Memphis, on his first leave from the Navy base in Norfolk, where he was stationed in 1936-37. Later he would be transferred up to Annapolis, and that was how his mother Carrie and his aunt Bessie would eventually move up to the Maryland area, where McCormick found them. Louis was very close to his uncle [Robert], and in fact, when McCormick visited Carrie in 1972, was so disturbed by the conversation that he retreated into his room and refused to come out.
>
> And the other man in the picture? The man in the sharp pin-striped suit? That, of course, is Robert Johnson. I stare and stare

at the picture, study it, scrutinize it, seek to memorize it, and for my very efforts I am defeated. What is there in this face, this expression; what can you read into a photograph? The man has short nappy hair; he is slight, one foot is raised, and he is up on his toes as though stretching for height. There is a sharp crease in his pants, and a handkerchief protrudes from his breast pocket — real or imaginary, I'm no longer sure: perhaps it would be more accurate to say that the *image* of a handkerchief protrudes. His eyes are deep-set, reserved, his expression forms a half-smile, there seems to be a gentleness about him, his fingers are extraordinarily long and delicate, his head is tilted to one side. That is all. There may well be more, but that is all I can remember.

CHAPTER 12

THE COMPLETE RECORDINGS DEFIES SALES PREDICTIONS

John Hammond once said, "When I was selecting talent for my first 'Spirituals to Swing' concert, I sent for Robert Johnson. I wanted black music to make an impression on a white audience and we got the finest exponents of blues, jazz and gospel music that we could find. Can you imagine how famous Robert Johnson would be today had he been able to make it?"

Based on the sales figures of *Robert Johnson: King of the Delta Blues Singers Volumes I and II* in 1961 and 1970, respectively, it is easy to understand how Hammond could have made such a statement. No one, Hammond included, could have predicted that when Johnson was finally reissued in the compact disc format in 1990 and people finally had the opportunity to see what this legendary blues artist actually looked like, that over one million units would be sold around the world and that the music and image of Johnson would become an integral part of American music history, on par with the legacies of such African-American artists as Louis Armstrong, Duke Ellington, John Coltrane and Miles Davis.

After years of allowing metal parts and tapes to languish in vaults and arbitrating disputes over who owned the rights to the Johnson photographs, Columbia Records decided to forge ahead and issue a deluxe box set that contained not only all 29 of Johnson's previously issued recordings, but his alternate takes as well. At the time, this amounted to 41 tracks to be released on three LPs, two cassette tapes, or two CDs (an unreleased alternate take of "Traveling Riverside Blues" was discovered at the Library of Congress after the release of the box set).

Steve LaVere was determined to be the legal copyright holder of the compositions and photographs and was selected to write the liner notes and supply lyric transcriptions to be included in the packaging of the box set, which was eventually called *Robert Johnson: The Complete Recordings*. Columbia had created a new label to handle its older, archival material. The label, called Legacy, had developed a *Roots'N Blues* series, and the Johnson box set was to be the flag-waver in its inaugural release.

No record company executive in his wildest dreams could have foreseen the explosion of sales of blues recordings more than 50 years old after the release of *The Complete Recordings*. Virtually every music-related magazine in the U.S. and abroad ran a feature story on the box set, not to mention stories in the daily newspapers and on network news. The box set capitalized on an untapped vein of interest no one knew was there. By 1994 the Recording Industry Association of America (RIAA) had certified *The Complete Recordings* with more than one million unit sales, earning the box set a Platinum Award, something no other blues reissue had ever achieved. Earlier, in 1991, the set won a Grammy Award for Best Historical Recording.

Johnson, so little known in his lifetime, was reborn in the public consciousness, with the t-shirts, posters and other marketing paraphernalia to prove it. Such was his ascendancy after the phenomenal and unexpected success of *The Complete Recordings* that Johnson was chosen for one of the highest honors that can be bestowed posthumously upon an American of great cultural influence — a commemorative stamp. Commemorative postage stamps are typically issued with great fanfare and media exposure and are on daily display to the millions of Americans who do business at a post office. Because a commemorative stamp is a sort of historical seal of approval from the government of the United States, the honorees are chosen with the utmost seriousness and are thoroughly vetted by the august Citizens' Stamp Advisory Committee.

The selection process has proven contentious at times — witness the years-long wrangling over Elvis Presley. A small but vocal constituency didn't consider Elvis enough of a model American citizen to deserve the honor of a postage stamp. They pointed to his alleged (and well-documented) drug abuse and occasional bad-boy behavior as reasons to exclude him from consideration. Millions of Elvis fans felt otherwise and demanded a commemorative stamp. The USPS waved a flag of surrender. After an unparalleled media blitz by the Postal Service, a youthful image of Elvis was chosen by popular vote over a Las Vegas-era image of an older Elvis. Although commemorative stamps are issued only within a specified time frame, the long-out-of-print Elvis stamps today still fetch steep prices among collectors, as eBay will attest.

Biographers had so little information to go on with Johnson that questions regarding his character were not at issue. What was at issue was the cigarette hanging out of his mouth.

The Johnson stamp was one of eight issued in the *Legends of American Music Series: Jazz Singers/Blues Singers* commemorative series in 1994. Besides Johnson there were stamp portraits of Bessie Smith, Muddy Waters, Billie Holiday, Jimmy Rushing, "Ma" Rainey, Mildred Bailey and Howlin' Wolf. Of the eight stamps the only one that generated any controversy was the one of Johnson, which was based on the dime-store self-portrait that featured Johnson with a cigarette stuck between his lips.

Artist Julian Allen was asked by the CSAC to remove the cigarette from his original portrait. He complied, removing the offending item with his painter's brush. He later remarked that the assignment was "one of the toughest I've ever done."[13] However, the original illustration, created in oil, was faithful to the dime-store photograph. The only creative license Allen took was changing the rumpled fabric background in the photograph to a weathered wood, as is typically seen on the shotgun shacks that populate the Mississippi Delta.

The CSAC was quoted in the media saying it asked for the cigarette's removal because "they didn't want the stamps to be perceived as promoting cigarettes." When the stamps were officially unveiled on September 17, 1994, at the Mississippi Delta Blues Festival in Greenwood, Miss., an immediate hue and cry went up from thousands of blues fans who felt that the specter of political correctness had compromised the integrity of the image. Thomas Humber of the National Smokers Alliance fired off a letter to Postmaster General Marvin Runyon in which he fumed (perhaps literally) that the decision to remove the cigarette was "an affront to the more than 50 million Americans who choose to smoke … [it] takes political correctness to a new height … placing it above historical accuracy."

Another writer complained that the stamp "didn't end up with an image with one less object in it; it ended up with a different image — and a different Robert Johnson." Even non-smokers largely felt the tampering candy-coated the image of the "real" Johnson and was at cross-purposes with his music.

What did Stephen LaVere, who licensed and approved the portrait, have to say about the alteration? "It doesn't bother me at all," he said. "The postage stamp is not supposed to be the photograph. The photo was just a guide to the artist. I don't consider that an offense in any way."

The stamp sold well in spite of the missing cigarette and, like the Elvis stamps, is today treasured by both stamp collectors and

---

[13]The original photograph and the postage stamp can be viewed at http://www.photobooth.net/mt/archives/2005/03/24/robert_johnson_photobooth_controversy.php

music fans. The tempest over the stamp and the ensuing publicity didn't hurt sales of *The Complete Recordings* either. By 1995 few Americans hadn't encountered Johnson — previously an all-but-forgotten blues singer from the 1930s — in some form or fashion, even if they didn't always recognize the name.

CHAPTER 13

A SON IS FOUND

In 1984 a gravel truck driver named Claud Johnson from Crystal Springs, Miss., dropped in at the office of attorney Jim Kitchens in the city of Jackson. Kitchens and Claud Johnson had known each other for more than 30 years, from the days when Claud had delivered goods to the Kitchens' family store in Crystal Springs. But, as reporter Ellen Barry of the *Los Angeles Times* related the conversation, Claud Johnson had something on his mind that day:

> He [Claud] walked in one day and said, "Jim, do you know who Robert Johnson was?"
> I said, "Sure I do," Kitchens recalled.
> He said, "How do you know that?"
> I said, "I listen to public radio."
> He said, "That was my daddy."
> I said, "What?"
> He said, "That was my daddy."
> I said, "Who else knows this?"
> He said, "Well, there's my momma."

Claud Johnson had known he was the son of a blues singer named Robert Johnson pretty much his whole life. He knew his mother, Virgie Mae Smith, had been 17 years old when she gave birth to him out of wedlock. Because his mother was so young when he was born, his maternal grandparents spent the most time raising him. They never tried to hide the fact that his father was Robert Johnson.

Claud's grandfather was a preacher and sharecropper who thought blues was the devil's music and would not allow it to be played or sung in his house. Claud recalled for a reporter how he remembered seeing Robert Johnson just twice when he came by for a visit. His grandparents would not allow the bluesman in the house or even up on their front porch. He was made to stand in the yard where he talked to them for a few minutes and left, never to return.

Claud told *New York Times* reporter Rick Bragg that his father seemed "clean-cut" and was "sharply dressed."

"I was fortunate," he told Bragg. "At least I got to see him."

His mother later married a man named Marshall Cain and changed Claud's last name accordingly. When Claud was grown, however, he legally changed his last name to Johnson. His first Social Security card, he claims, carried that name.

Claud Johnson was content to live his quiet life and go about his business with his gravel truck until the day he received a summons to appear in court about litigation over the establishment of the legitimate heirs to the Estate of Robert Johnson. Stephen LaVere, the music historian who had found Carrie Thompson, Johnson's half-sister, and through her the only known photographs of Johnson, had steadfastly maintained and overseen the once worthless Estate of Johnson until it had amassed well over a million dollars in licensing fees and royalties. LaVere accomplished this by copyrighting the two Johnson photographs and charging a fee for each use. More significantly, he formally copyrighted Johnson's songs, which had been considered by many musicians up to that time as being in the public domain and free for anyone's use.[14] Platinum-selling artists such as Eric Clapton, the Rolling Stones and Led Zeppelin were asked to pony-up back royalties to Johnson

---

[14]The songs were never part of the public domain. They were covered by common law copyright, which meant that Robert Johnson's heirs owned the rights to the works. However, the formal copyright gave his heirs and LaVere the power to bring legal action and to obtain monetary damages from anyone who violates the copyright law.

songs they had made famous, and, it should be noted, used without charge.

Not all were happy when LaVere came knocking. Some, such as Eric Clapton, willingly and cheerfully paid the royalties due. Others, such as the Rolling Stones, weren't so open with their purse strings. At any rate, the money began to pour in with half going to LaVere's company, and the other half held in trust until the courts could determine the rightful heirs. The fifty-fifty arrangement LaVere had with Carrie Thompson and her heirs (she died in 1983 and left her share of Johnson's Estate to two others) not surprisingly got a lot messier when the Johnson Estate reached the million dollar mark.

Word that Johnson had an illegitimate son had circulated among the blues cognoscenti for years after blues historian Mack McCormick had discovered Virgie Mae Smith in Crystal Springs while retracing the known travels of Johnson. According to McCormick, Smith happily volunteered the information about her intimacies with Johnson and the subsequent birth of her son Claud. The court-appointed administrator of the Johnson Estate was tipped off by LaVere that a son possibly existed. Soon after, Claud Johnson and his mother, who was still living, were summoned to testify.

In a sworn deposition in 1992, Virgie Mae Smith (Cain) testified that Claud Johnson was, in fact, the son of bluesman Robert L. Johnson and that she and Johnson had conceived the child in the woods on her way to school in 1931. She further claimed that other than Johnson, she had no other sexual partner during that period of time. Even though the evidence clearly showed that Claud had legally changed his last name to Johnson long before anyone thought money was to be made off the bluesman, corroborating the sexual liaison that supposedly took place in 1931 still was not going to be easy.

It was at this point, in 1998, that the lawyers decided to bring in a friend of Virgie Mae Smith's who had been close to her since they were children. Her name was Eula Mae Williams and she claimed to have witnessed the conception of Claud Johnson. Which is another way of saying she had watched Johnson and Virgie Mae Smith have sex in the woods. What follows is the transcript of what Williams had to say about it all:

Finally, Claud offered the deposition testimony of Eula Mae Williams, another childhood friend of Virgie Mae. The eighty-year old Williams testified that she and Claud's mother were friends before, during, and after the time Virgie Mae became pregnant. Eula Mae testified that she and Virgie Mae grew up in the same crossroads community in Copiah County and, as young girls, attended community events together. They shared secrets and obviously relied upon one another for support and companionship. They were also prone to sneak out to "house parties" where they would listen to the music of various blues musicians. It was at one of these celebrations that Virgie Mae met Johnson. Contrary to Virgie Mae's assertion that no one ever saw Johnson and her engage in sexual intercourse, Eula Mae testified that she did in fact see Virgie Mae and Johnson engage in sexual intercourse in the spring prior to Claud's birth in December. The resulting courtship is best expressed by Eula Mae herself in response to pretrial questioning by attorney Victor McTeer, wherein Eula Mae described an incident where she, her boyfriend, Virgie Mae, and Johnson all went for a "walk" in the spring of 1931:

Q: All right, so you walked off the road, correct?

A: Right.

Q: And you started to kiss and do whatever people do?

A: M-hm.

Q: All right. Now, when you started that, what was Virgie and—

A: Doing the same thing we were.

Q: How do you know? You were sitting there watching them while you were —

A: We was both standing up.

Q: Oh, so both of you were standing up in the woods?

A: Sure, we was standing up out there in the woods.

Q: Excuse me, I haven't finished yet. Virgie and Robert, were they kissing and standing up?

A: Right.

Q: Was there ever a time when you were not looking at them?

A: Well, yes.

Q: I see. Did you at any point in time remove your clothing?

A: Well, had to.

Q: Okay. Did you observe them remove their clothing?

A: Sure.

Q: You were sitting there watching someone else do this?

A: I done told you.

Q: Well, let me, let me share something with you, because I'm really curious about this. Maybe I have a more limited experience. But you're saying to me that you were watching them make love?

A: M-hm.

Q: While you were making love?

A: M-hm.

Q: You don't think that's at all odd?

A: Say what?

Q: Have you ever done that before or since?

A: Yes.

Q: Watch other people make love?

A: Yes, I have done it before. Yes, I've done it after I married. Yes.

Q: You watched other people make love?

A: Yes, sir. Yes, sir.

Q: Other than ... other than Mr. Johnson and Virgie Cain.

A: Right.

Q: Really?

A: You haven't?

Q: No. Really haven't.

A: I'm sorry for you.

Q: Well, I appreciate that. And perhaps I need the wealth of experience that you have. But share with me this. Did you actually watch them engage in the act? You actually watched that?

A: Yes.

Q: When they were engaging in the act, was your husband (her boyfriend at the time) watching, too?

A: Sure.

Q: Okay. Did they watch you?

A: Sure.

Q: And you watched them watch you?
A: Yes.

Eula Mae also testified that Virgie Mae told her she was pregnant with Johnson's baby in May of 1931, the year of Claud's birth. Moreover, Eula Mae testified as follows about a chance meeting with Johnson several years after Claud's birth:

Q: Now, ma'am, when you saw R. L. Johnson there at Shelby some years after Claud's birth, did you talk to him at all?
A: Yes, we talked about the baby.
Q: Tell us about that conversation. ...
A: Well, I was just asking when was he coming back down here. He said, "Well, I'm not coming back." He said, "I'm going pretty good right now." He say, "I'll be up here." He said, "She done got married now, and she got a husband and children."

The court ruled that Claud was Johnson's son.

The gravel truck operator inherited over a million dollars and now lives on a large estate he bought in the town of Crystal Springs, Miss., his hometown. Other than that and the Robert Johnson fans who show up from time to time, not a whole lot else has changed for him. Curiously, Claud Johnson reports that if he leaves a drink before he has finished it he will not touch it later. He is superstitious that way. He is afraid of being poisoned.

CHAPTER 14

THE 3.5-SECOND PIECE OF CELLULOID

S andbagged. Ambushed. That's the way Leo Allred, better known among blues enthusiasts and Beale Street patrons as Tater Red, felt by the time a panel of Robert Johnson experts had worked him over at the Rock and Roll Hall of Fame in Cleveland, Ohio, in 1998.

All the fuss and commotion was over a 3.5-second piece of celluloid that, to a whole lot of people, looked a whole lot like Robert Leroy Johnson, The King of the Delta Blues. An audience full of blues luminaries — including Robert Jr. Lockwood and Henry Townsend, both of whom had known Johnson, as well as scholars, writers and researchers, among them Peter Guralnick and Steve LaVere — were there for a showing and discussion of this momentary glimpse of a black street musician playing guitar and blowing on a rack harmonica.

It all began when a group of loosely associated friends that included Tater Red discovered a cache of old 16 mm film footage left behind in the projection room of the Delta Theater in the tiny town of Ruleville, Miss. Tater Red's grandmother had worked at the theater and knew that the theater's owner, Bem Jackson, many decades ago had shot 16 mm silent film footage of daily life in the Ruleville area — activities such as football games, street fairs, happenings in and around the Delta — and shown the films at his theater, which thrilled audience members who delighted in seeing themselves bigger than life on a movie screen.

A decision was made some years later to transfer as much of the surviving film stock as possible to video to preserve it for posterity. A master video was made, and copies were struck and distributed to a wide circle of friends and acquaintances from the Ruleville area, including Tater Red.

One night, as he watched the video, a 3.5 second street scene stopped him cold. "That guy sure looks familiar," Tater Red thought to himself as he paused and repeated the brief segment over and over again. "Is it? — Nah, it couldn't be. Maybe it is. It sure looks like him." He located photos of Johnson in his CD collection and began to compare them with what was on the video. "I think it might be him," he decided.

Tater Red was no stranger to blues or to Johnson. He was familiar to thousands of radio listeners in the Mid-South for a weekly blues show he had hosted for years on one of Memphis' top-rated commercial radio stations. He also had made a radical entrepreneurial move on Beale Street, which had long been criticized for its second-rate tourist shops and tepid, predictable blues clubs that showcased tepid, predictable blues artists. Authentic was not a word that instantly leapt to mind when strolling down this most famed of Memphis streets.

Tater Red opened Tater Red's Lucky Mojos, a shop that offered some of the weirdest, wackiest and ultimately coolest souvenirs and bric-a-brac to be found in the whole tourist district. Need some Shut Your Mouth oil? Tater Red has it. Some of that John the Conquerer Root you heard about in a blues song? Got that, too. Goofer dust. Of course. Other Lawyer Be Stupid soap? Mm-hmm. Plus many other spells, potions, elixirs, voodoo dolls, black cat bones, Mexican saints wallets — not to mention a zany assortment of t-shirts and hats. No real blues fan can possibly escape without loosening the wallet for something.[15]

Knowing full well the interest that a film segment of Johnson might likely attract, Tater Red duplicated a frame from the video

---

[15] See for yourself at www.taterreds.com

of the 16 mm footage and had it blown up. He circulated a few prints to people he knew to gauge opinion. The verdict was near unanimous: It was either Robert Johnson or someone who was a dead ringer. The photograph was shown, reportedly, to Robert Jr. Lockwood and other bluesmen who had known Johnson and the answer almost always came back the same. "It's him!" they declared without hesitation.

Word spread quickly to the world press about the film clip and articles were hastily written "describing things that weren't in it by people who had never seen it," according to Tater Red. There were endless phone calls, inquiries, visitations, reporters and, naturally, legal woes. According to Tater Red, Jimmy Page and Robert Plant of Led Zeppelin came into his shop, moseyed around for about three hours then finally put the question to him about the video. He obliged and showed it to them. Like so many others, they were absolutely convinced it was Johnson. They half-jokingly asked if the film were for sale and with a wink offered to pay a million dollars for it. Tater Red laughed and told them it wasn't for sale, that many people already owned copies of the video.

The Rolling Stones followed suit, contacting Tater Red and clamoring for the video themselves. The press soon reported that six and seven figure sums had been offered for the footage. Tater Red eventually grew weary of all the hoo-hah and referred others to the archives at the Center for the Study of Southern Culture at Ole Miss, where Bem Jackson's family had donated the original archival film footage. "It became a nightmare," says Tater Red.

In 1998 the respected writer and critic Robert Santelli in his role as Education Director for the Rock and Roll Hall of Fame invited Tater Red to a symposium on Johnson that was part of a week-long celebration of the musician. A panel of experts had been asked to examine the 3.5 seconds of footage and render a verdict on whether the bluesman in question was Johnson. Distinguished documentarian Robert Mugge was there to capture it all on film.

The cameras were rolling, the lights were blazing, the microphones humming. Tater Red Allred sat in the audience. He had not been invited on the stage.

Bem Jackson's vintage footage was shown, the speakers made their declarations, and blues historian and attorney Tom Freeland stood at the lectern for what seemed to be a fully planned and programmed PowerPoint presentation. *Click, buzz, zoom* — the projector paused and swooped into a high-tech close-up of a movie poster barely discernable in a display box on the outside of the Delta Theater. If your eyes were following the Johnson-like figure in the foreground, you would never notice the film poster in the background. Freeland, as well as LaVere, obviously, noticed. The movie being shown at the theater that day, as advertised on a movie poster shown in an impressive PowerPoint juxtaposition, was *Blues in the Night*, which was released in 1941, three years after Johnson was laid to rest. Ergo, the bluesman in the film clip couldn't be Johnson because Johnson was dead. End of story.

But not for Tater Red. He was given a microphone and put on the spot about the claim for the footage being Johnson, as if he were somehow to blame. Visibly flustered, he tries to explain that he had no way of verifying the footage, that, hey, he was just as curious as everyone else. A question posed to Robert Jr. Lockwood by the moderator, Bob Santelli, about rumors he had authenticated the footage privately brought a thundering denunciation from Lockwood. All in all, it wasn't a happy day for Tater Red.

Now that a decade has passed since the big showdown in Cleveland, what does Tater Red have to say about it all?

"It ain't him."

And so the question stands: If it's not Johnson, then just who is it? Again, silence. No one has come forward with a positive identification. In the mythology of Robert Johnson, the 3.5 seconds of film footage was simply another blind alley, another windswept journey with no seeming end or resolution.

LEGENDS LIVE ON

When I first began research on this book, I interviewed renowned blues historian Dr. David Evans. He gave me a polite warning that at this stage of the game I wasn't likely to uncover any new information about Robert Johnson. True enough. There probably isn't a single county courthouse in all of Mississippi that hasn't been double-teamed by researchers seeking that one missing document pertaining to the bluesman. Documentary film crews have aimed their cameras at virtually everyone who ever knew the man, and yet the portrait remains frustratingly incomplete.

Since Johnson's death there has seemed to be a mathematical equation of sorts at play: The less truth we have, the more myth we get. Johnson has in fact become a figure of American mythology, not unlike the fictional Pecos Bill or Paul Bunyan or the real-life Davy Crockett or Billy the Kid. Robert Johnson? Isn't he the bluesman who sold his soul to the devil at the crossroads and died after being poisoned by a jealous husband? To millions of people, undoubtedly these associations will be the ones that endure.

To researchers the trail has gone cold in many ways. Most of Johnson's contemporaries are now dead, and those few still living often demand a briefcase full of money to speak a few words about him. If anything, my own journey into Johnson's world has produced a tale that is reductive rather than expansive. The more details we get — and there are a lot of details, most of them unverified, about Johnson — the less we truly seem to know him. Johnny Shines arguably spent more time with Johnson than any other bluesman, yet knew practically nothing about his life other than what he observed first hand. In interview after interview Shines, who was an articulate and thoughtful man, had difficulty putting his finger on just who his friend really was and what he was all about.

As a man, Johnson was all too human with all-too-human weaknesses. The combination of his vices of women and alcohol may have been his undoing. As an artist, however, his stature has grown, his myth ever-pervasive in the American consciousness. The loss of his first wife may have taken an immeasurable emotional toll on Johnson, but it is difficult to reconcile this grief with the callous disdain he had for his second wife. These contradictions seem to be a part of what forged Johnson into the enigma he was and remains and, in turn, his great art — the poetic paranoia threaded into his songs, the sense of loss and pain so urgently evoked in his lyrics, the world of darkness and shadows that seemed to torment him.

Until Gayle Dean Wardlow found the death certificate, many researchers had thought Johnson was a far younger man when he died. As it is, Johnson was the founding member of the so-called 27 Club. Robert Johnson, Brian Jones, Janis Joplin, Jimi Hendrix, Jim Morrison, Kurt Cobain — all dead at the age of 27.

And the final coincidence? Johnson died on August 16, the same day as Elvis Presley.

Their legends live on.

Appendix, Bibliography and Index

A BRIEF DISCUSSION OF JOHNSON'S MUSIC

This addendum will take a detour from our narrative to briefly describe some of the music of Robert Johnson without the benefit of a CD and without knowing if the reader has ever actually heard Johnson — or Delta blues for that matter.

Johnson recorded 29 songs in his lifetime and it would ill-suit our purposes here to describe each song and each of the extant 42 takes in numbing detail. There are other books out there that do a fine job of dissecting every verse and stanza Johnson ever wrote and enough guitar transcriptions floating around on the Internet to keep guitar players busy for months. So we will take the approach of mentioning a few specifics and a few generalities and hope the reader will be enticed into digging deeper on his or her own.

So, if you've never heard him, what does Johnson actually sound like? In a word, *old*. An unaccompanied singer/guitarist — with no back-up band, no ear-blasting volume, no samples, no bass thunder, no drum to kick out a dance beat — all sounds hopelessly old-fashioned and outdated to the untutored ear. With all the electronic studio effects available to today's performers, Johnson's music is all the more striking because it is stripped clean of all artifice and additives — it is laid bare, naked to the flesh. It is exactly that raw, bone deep, unfiltered emotion that seems to stir some fathomless *something* in so many listeners, and it is that indefinable *something*, that *feeling*, that makes so many writers want to call Johnson's music art. In few words and few lines Johnson conjures a whole personal universe that comes alive in his listener's mind.

Johnson is most definitely an acquired taste for those who have grown up in a culture dominated by layered multi-tracking and a symphony of beats, but it is precisely those dramatic pauses, those silences and flourishes, those vocal nuances and punctuations that make Johnson's music seem all the more intimate and real, that pull you in close, as if he is pouring out all his sorrows and terror-filled imaginings just for you.

In an age of noise pollution and music systems measured by wattage, it is an indication of Johnson's artistic greatness that the "white space" in his sound is such an attraction. Although modern technology has reportedly done wonders for the crackly, tinny sound of Johnson's original pressings and metal parts, they still sound decidedly low-fi. Johnson sat in front of a single microphone to capture both his vocal and instrumental playing, unlike today where he would be recorded with at least two microphones and probably would record vocals and instruments separately on separate tracks. In 1936 and 1937 this wasn't technically possible. Recording was done live in the studio, typically in double takes. You either got it or you didn't.

The novice listener may not be as well served by Johnson's 42 tracks, many of which are second takes, on the exhaustive *The Complete Recordings* as the hardcore fans who want to hear every note. The first-time listener may be best acclimated by obtaining the new superior-sounding 17-track CD version of the original *King of the Delta Blues Singers*, the album that kicked Johnson's legacy into high gear when released by Columbia Records in 1961. Those songs, it should be remembered, are what cemented Johnson's legacy in the world consciousness.

To give you, the reader, some sense of Johnson's many different songs and styles, three specific tracks have been selected for a more microscopic examination. These three songs represent a cross-section of Johnson's talent, from the poetic verve of his lyrics to his dazzling musicianship to his emotive vocal flights to his musical diversity, as well as his song crafting ability. The songs we will zoom in on, so to speak, are: "Preaching Blues (Up Jumped the Devil)," "They're Red Hot," and "Love In Vain Blues." Each represents an important, different facet of Johnson.

PREACHING BLUES (UP JUMPED THE DEVIL)

As writer Elijah Wald observed, "Preaching Blues" with its added parentheses and the words "up jumped the devil" was the first of Johnson's supposed satanic references in any song, but oddly, the lyrics offer no further mention of the devil. Instead Johnson gives the listener his definition of what blues is: "a low-down shakin' chill" and "like consumption (ed. — tuberculosis) killing me by degrees." He also tells us he has the blues and hopes we, the listeners, won't have the misfortune to get them.

The song was not Johnson's own. It was originally written and recorded by his blues traveler friend and mentor Son House, but like most re-recorded blues tunes, Johnson extensively reworked both music and lyrics making the piece very much his own. Like hip-hop artists of today who sample a surprising variety of snippets from all walks of music, Delta blues artists freely borrowed from each other's bags of tricks and bent the songs to their own will. The more visionary the artist, the more likely he would want to reshape the work to his own artistic purpose.

"Preaching Blues" was one of the two songs John Hammond chose to play at Carnegie Hall for the "From Spirituals to Swing" concert. As engaging as the lyrics are, it is the breathtaking guitar playing and fast beat that make "Preaching Blues" one of Johnson's more accessible songs for today's audiences. The song begins with a standard slow blues walk-down, then surprises the listener after a few beats by stopping cold and picking up a sinuous, new thumping beat with a slide guitar snaking all over the song. It's a challenging song for even the nimblest picker and a benchmark of sorts for the beginning guitar player hoping to master Johnson's chops. Several musicians have commented on the clarity of

Johnson's hyperkinetic playing, something very difficult to achieve under the best of circumstances, but doubly hard when you are under the pressure of recording and playing at breakneck speed. This song was, apparently, nailed in one take.

"Preaching Blues" also features some of Johnson's most expressive and energized vocals. In spite of warning the listener about getting a case of the blues, his vocal style is one of barely contained frenzy, and, in fact, he starts his singing with a high-pitched eerie moan, "Mmmm mmmm." He surprises the listener yet again, lowering his voice into a gutbucket growl for a few lines then returning to his natural singing voice. He even talks to himself between verses, prodding himself: "You gon' do it? / Tell me all about it."

One can only imagine what the high-toned Carnegie Hall audience must have thought as this song raced through the sound system way back in 1938. It's a song that can still raise goose flesh with its unbridled power.

THEY'RE RED HOT

"They're Red Hot" is considered by many "Robert Johnsonologists" to be the least among his recordings, but in some ways it tells us the most. "Red Hot" stands separate from the rest of the Johnson canon by dint of the fact that it sounds like nothing else he recorded. It is a novelty song, a patchwork of mildly risqué hokum lyrics, old workhorses sung for easy laughs such as "Me and my babe bought a V-8 Ford / Well, we wind that thing all on the runnin' board. ..." Today's listeners, when they can puzzle out such obscure lyrics, barely raise an eyebrow over such timid naughtiness. But in the world of the 1930s such lyrics were sure-fire to juice up a juke-joint crowd.

The song is pure nonsense and delightfully so. The refrain is repeated through the song at least a dozen times: "Hot tamales and they red hot / yes, she got 'em for sale." The song is infectious, sung with total abandon by Johnson who clearly relishes the song.

All the writers who poured over the torture and torment they imagined in all the other Johnson songs came up against a brick wall with "Red Hot."

It is played full-throttle with fire and gusto, his voice sliding on occasion into gravelly inflection then back to his keening high tenor. One can easily imagine Johnson standing on a street corner, grinning to beat the devil, and drawing an eager crowd of coin tossers. Johnson, it should be remembered, was a working musician who earned his livelihood by his wits and his ability to sell himself to an audience.

Believe it or not, a nickel in 1936 could buy a man a small bite to eat. A hatful of coins was serious money. As previously discussed, Johnson tailored his song list to his audience. Those who were willing to pay him a nickel or dime to play a popular cowboy song instead of a blues would most certainly have had their request honored. He would have been foolish to do otherwise. Up-tempo songs like "Red Hot," sung primarily, one would have to assume, to adult crowds not only at juke joints but at medicine shows, fish fries, rent parties and even the election campaigns of whites from time to time, made people want to laugh, dance and just *shake it*. This song is a clue to the jubilant, high-fiving Johnson his friends spoke of. Johnson may have been quiet, introverted, moody, maybe even depressed at times, and these characteristics are reflected in some of his songs. But "Red Hot" proves that Johnson had a lighter side and knew how to work a crowd and make the ladies blush.

This was a talent he was to put to good use until his dying day.

LOVE IN VAIN BLUES

If any one song of Robert Johnson's can be held up as a thing of beauty and timeless art, it is "Love In Vain Blues," famously covered by the Rolling Stones on their *Let It Bleed* album prior to the reissue of the song in 1970 on *King of the Delta Blues Singers Vol. II*. Very few people had heard the original 78 of the song, and to millions of Rolling Stones fans, the song was a revelation. Interest in Johnson at that point took a quantum leap.

"Love In Vain Blues" is a slow blues, a tale of sadness and slow-motion heartbreak as a man sees his woman to the train station and watches in silence as her train departs. He confesses to the listener, "I was lonesome / and I could not help but cry." It was a scene played out millions of times in America during the golden age of public train transportation. As his woman leaves him, the song's narrator feels abandoned, as if all the love in his heart was "in vain," hopeless, wasted. He comments that after the train leaves, all that is left is the "two lights on behind" of the train's caboose, an indelible visual image.

What makes the song so intimate and moving, besides the brooding vocal of Johnson, is the subtle but palpable sense of dread he imparts to ordinary details of travel and separation. When he tells of bringing his woman to the station "with a suitcase in my hand" followed by the words "Well, it's hard to tell, it's hard to tell/ When all your love's in vain," we can instantly imagine what is set to happen next. When he then tells us "I looked her in the eye" and "could not help but cry" we sense a man who is falling apart inside.

Technically the song is not wholly original — it takes "suggestions" from works by Blind Lemon Jefferson and Leroy Carr — but it might as well be, so reshaped and retooled are the words and music. The result is an almost seamless combination of elements — minimalist accents from the guitar, the weary tone of voice, the intimate pull of the lyrics — that coalesce into a whole, a song of transcendence and pain.

The last verse is curious for a number of reasons. It closes with the final words "All my love's in vain," but is otherwise hummed and moaned except for the name "Willie Mae" that he utters twice, obviously the name of the woman who left him behind at the train station. The moans and cries of the final verse clearly indicate the singer's anguish.

An interesting footnote to the song is that the lady in question, Willie Mae Cross, who was a cousin of bluesman David "Honeyboy" Edwards, was actually found living in the Mississippi Delta and was interviewed for the documentary films *Can't You Hear the Wind Howl?* and *The Search for Robert Johnson* where she reminisces about her fleeting time spent with Johnson. At one point, with a twinkle in her eye, she tells the interviewer that Johnson was "the cutest little brown thing you ever seen." One of the highlights of the films is when Willie Mae listens to a recording of "Love In Vain Blues." A memory frozen in time seems to flash across her now lined and aged face when she hears Johnson sing her name and a shy smile slowly plays on her lips. It is a priceless moment.

NOTES

Greil Marcus, in his critically acclaimed book *Mystery Train*, states that three unrecorded Johnson songs have been covered by other artists. Robert Jr. Lockwood recorded the songs "Little Boy Blue" and "Take A Little Walk With Me" in 1941, which were later released on an Austrian import LP, *Mississippi Country Blues – Vol. 1, 1935-1951* (Document 519). Johnny Shines released the song "Tell Me Mama" on his 1972 LP *Sitting On Top of the World* (Biograph 12044). These tracks are now available on several compact disc compilations.

Steve LaVere copyrighted two unrecorded Johnson songs based on testimony from Lockwood and Shines. Lockwood informed LaVere that he learned "Mr. Down Child" from Johnson and that it was a song Johnson wrote but didn't record. The Shines one, of course, is "Tell Me Mama," but there's also "Louisiana Blues," which Shines attributed to Johnson. Most authorities also believe that all four of Lockwood's Bluebird label tunes - "Take a Little Walk with Me" (a clone of "Sweet Home Chicago"), "Little Boy Blue," "Black Spider Blues" and "I'm Gonna Train My Baby" were derived from Johnson originals.

A compelling and intriguing case is made on the Web site www.touched.co.uk/press/rjnote.html that Johnson's music was recorded at least 20 percent too fast. There are many pros and cons to the argument and, indeed, many recordings over the years have been speeded-up to make them seem livelier. The Web site listed offers several samples of Johnson songs slowed down, and they make for some very interesting listening. An unauthorized U.K. compact disc, *Steady Rollin' Man*, is available that contains 24 Johnson songs slowed down to what the reissuers consider the "correct" speed. It should be noted that none of Johnson's contemporaries ever mentioned that his recordings sounded too fast or unnatural.

BIBLIOGRAPHY

Amick, George. *U.S. Stamp Yearbook 1994*. Sidney, Ohio: Linn's Stamp News, 1995.

Associated Press. "High Blood Pressure Killed Booker T. Washington." 7 May 2006.

Associated Press. "Lost Letter Reveals Tales of Legendary Bluesman Robert Johnson." 9 Jan. 2006.

Barry, Ellen. "Bluesman's Son Gets His Due." *Los Angeles Times*. 2 June 2004.

Blesh, Rudi. *Shining Trumpets: A History of Jazz*. New York: Knopf, 1946.

Booth, Stanley. *Rythm Oil: A Journey Through the Music of the American South*. New York: Pantheon Books, 1991.

Bragg, Rick. "Court Rules Father of the Blues Has a Son." Associated Press. 17 June 2000.

Calt, Stephen and Gayle Dean Wardlow. *King of the Delta Blues: The Life and Music of Charley Patton*. Newton, New Jersey: Rock Chapel Press, 1988.

Charters, Sam. *The Country Blues*. New York: Rinehardt Co., 1959.

Charters, Sam. "Seeking the Greatest Bluesman." *American Heritage*. July/Aug. 1991.

Connell, David. "Retrospective Blues: Robert Johnson — An Open Letter to Eric Clapton." *British Medical Journal*. 2 Sept. 2006.

Cohn, Lawrence, ed. *Nothing but the Blues*. New York: Abbeville, 1993.

Davis, Francis. *The History of the Blues: The Roots, the Music, the People from Charley Patton to Robert Cray*. New York: Hyperion, 1995.

DeCurtis, Anthony, James Henke, and Holly George-Warren, eds., *Rolling Stone Album Guide*. New York: Straight Arrow Publishers, 1992.

Delta Haze Corporation. "Robert Johnson." 14 Sept. 2005. www.deltahaze.com/johnson/Legacy.html

"Don Law." Country Music Hall of Fame on-line. 10 Feb. 2006. www.countrymusichalloffame.com/site/inductees.aspx?cid=137#

Driggs, Frank. Liner notes. *Robert Johnson, King of the Delta Blues Singers, Vol. I.* New York: Columbia Records, 1961.

Dylan, Bob. *Chronicles.* New York: Simon & Schuster, 2004.

Erlewine, Michael and Scott Bultman, eds. *All Music Guide.* San Francisco: Miller Freeman, 1992.

Evans, David. *Big Road Blues.* Berkeley: University of California Press, 1982.

Evans, David. *Tommy Johnson.* London: Studio Vista, 1971.

Gates, David. "Rescued from Oblivion." *The Oxford American.* Issue 27 and 28, 1999.

Gordon, Robert. *Can't Be Satisfied.* New York: Little, Brown and Company, 2002.

Gordon, Robert. "The Plundering of Robert Johnson." *L.A. Weekly.* 5-11 July 1991.

Guralnick, Peter. *Feel Like Going Home: Portraits in Blues and Rock 'n' Roll.* New York: Outerbridge & Dienstfrey, 1971.

Guralnick, Peter. *Lost Highway: Journeys and Arrivals of American Musicians.* New York: David R. Godine, Publishers, 1979.

Guralnick, Peter. *Searching for Robert Johnson.* New York: Obelisk Books/E.P.Dutton, 1989.

Guralnick, Peter. *Sweet Soul Music.* New York: Harper & Row, 1986.

Hall, Michael. "Mack McCormick Still Has the Blues." *Texas Monthly.* April, 2002.

Hammond, John. *John Hammond On Record.* New York: Summit Books, 1977.

Handy, W. C. *Father of the Blues.* New York: Collier Books, 1970.

Helm, Levon and Stephen Davis. *This Wheel's On Fire: Levon Helm and the Story of The Band.* New York: Morrow, 1994.

Holley, Donald. *The Second Great Emancipation: The Mechanical Cotton Picker, Black Migration, and How They Shaped the Modern South.* Fayetteville, Arkansas: University of Arkansas Press, 2000.

Howse, Pat and Jimmy Phillips. "Godfather of Delta Blues: An Interview with Gayle Dean Wardlow." *Peavey Monitor.* 1995.

Hunt, Chris. *The Search for Robert Johnson.* (TV film). Sony Music Corporation, 1992.

Kienzle, Rich. *Great Guitarists.* Pennsylvania: Facts On File, 1985.

Knopper, Steve. "Robert Johnson's Grave Found?" *Rolling Stone.* 12 Oct. 2000.

Knopper, Steve. "'Sweet Home Chicago' Leaves Sour Taste for Some." *Chicago Tribune.* 30 May 2002.

Lasker, Steven. "What Price Records? The U.S. Record Industry and the Retail Price of Popular Records, 1925-50." *VJM's Jazz and Blues Mart.* 2006. www.vjm.biz/new_page_11.htm.

LaVere, Stephen. Liner notes. *Robert Johnson: The Complete Recordings.* New York: CBS Records, Inc., 1990.

Leflore County (Mississippi) Chancery Court. Legal decision. "In the Supreme Court of Mississippi, No. 1998-CA-01573-SCT, In the Matter of the Estate of Robert L. Johnson, Deceased: Robert M. Harris and Annye C. Anderson vs. Claud L. Johnson." 15 Oct. 1998.

Lomax, Alan. *The Land Where the Blues Began.* New York: Pantheon Books, 1993.

Marcus, Greil. *Mystery Train: Images of America In Rock 'N' Roll Music.* New York: E.P. Dutton, 1975.

Marsh, Dave, ed. *The Rolling Stone Record Guide.* New York: Random House, 1979 and 1983.

Merrill, Buddy. May 2007. www.buddymerrillmusic.com

Meyer, Peter. *Can't You Hear the Wind Howl?* (Film). Winstar, 1998.

Mugge, Robert. *Hellhounds on My Trail: The Afterlife of Robert Johnson.* (Film). Winstar, 1999.

Nager, Larry. *Memphis Beat.* New York: St. Martin's Press, 1998.

Pareles, Jon and Patricia Romanowski, eds. *The Rolling Stone Encyclopedia of Rock & Roll.* New York, Summit Books, 1983.

Palmer, Robert. *Deep Blues.* New York: Viking, 1981.

Palmer, Robert. "King of the Delta Blues Singers." (Review). *Rolling Stone.* 18 Oct. 1990.

Pearson, Barry Lee and Bill McCullough. *Robert Johnson: Lost and Found.* Urbana and Chicago: University of Illinois Press, 2003.

Polizzotti, Mark. "Love In Vain." (Review). *New Republic.* 7 June 2004.

Wald, Elijah. *Escaping the Delta: Robert Johnson and the Invention of the Blues.* New York: Amistad, 2004.

Wardlow, Gayle Dean and Edward Komara. *Chasin' That Devil Music.* New York: Backbeat Books, 1998.

White, Timothy. "Time Traveling With Robert Johnson & Son." *Billboard.* 17 June 2000.

INDEX

A

B

C